CONTENTS

PUBLISHER'S NOTE

I felt particularly honored when Edmond Caruana, O.Carm., of the Libreria Editrice Vaticana offered us the possibility of producing an English translation of this text. He thought it would be a "good fit" inasmuch as the charism of our Priestly Society of John Henry Cardinal Newman is precisely to promote the theology and spirituality of that great convert, theologian, and churchman of the nineteenth century. Father Caruana also knew that the Reverend Nicholas L. Gregoris of our Community was both a Newman scholar and fluent in Italian. And so, with great enthusiasm we accepted this challenge, and I handed over the project to Father Gregoris with total confidence.

While the effort was deemed important, it was, all the same, a very formidable project, for an unforeseen reason. Father Velocci's work in Italian provides a most enjoyable "read," and Father Gregoris was certainly equal to the translation task. The difficulty arose from the realization that Father Velocci himself had had to translate his numerous citations from Newman's corpus and put them into Italian. Hence we were confronted with a double task: translating the Italian of Father Velocci into English and also moving his quotations from Newman back into Victorian English! An inestimable source of assistance in this work was Mrs. Jan Florick, who went about tracking down Newman's quotations with perseverance and devotion, thus helping to produce a text that is both faithful and readable.

In translating a work like this, certain stylistic decisions also had to be made. To minimize distractions, we have aimed to minimize inconsistencies in the published texts of Newman's writings as regards punctuation, spelling, and capitalization, while maintaining his precise language, for his theology is enshrined in and enhanced by his magnificent use of the English language. We have attempted to keep editorial notes to a minimum; and we have typeset Newman's own words in a distinctive font. For the most part, we have used the Longmans & Green editions of Newman's writings, and exceptions are noted.

A particularly welcome aspect of Father Velocci's book is the extensive use of Newman's own words. Thus, the author leads us on a tour through the Venerable Cardinal's thoughts on prayer; just as Saint John the Baptist lived to manifest Our Lord, Father Velocci always gives pride of place to Newman. Even a reader who is being newly introduced to Newman gets an excellent overview of Newman's mind and heart on prayer, as well as a comprehensive journey through dozens of primary documents. Perhaps best of all was Father Velocci's decision to include an appendix collecting several prayers of Cardinal Newman; we have added yet more examples of such prayers in the present edition.

The Foreword by Father Gregoris situates Newman's theology of prayer within that of other spiritual masters in the history of the Church.

For the reader not so familiar with Newman's biography, we have included an appendix of information about the Cardinal's life and work. This concise biographical sketch concludes with a prayer for the cause for Cardinal Newman's beatification and canonization; we hope that every reader of this book will render this service in gratitude for the Venerable Newman's tremendous service to the Church and the world, of his own age and of ours as well.

Rev. Peter M. J. Stravinskas

PRAYER IN NEWMAN

PRAYER IN NEWMAN

Giovanni Velocci, c.ss.r.

Translated, with a Foreword, by
Rev. Nicholas L. Gregoris

NEWMAN HOUSE PRESS

GRACEWING

Originally published as *La Preghiera in Newman*,
Libreria Editrice Vaticana, 2004

English translation copyright © 2006 Newman House Press
All rights reserved

Published in the United States of America by
Newman House Press
21 Fairview Avenue
Mount Pocono, Pennsylvania 18344

ISBN-10: 0-9778846-0-0
ISBN-13: 978-0-9778846-0-5

Published in the British Commonwealth and the European Union by
Gracewing Publishing, 2 Southern Avenue, Leominster
Herefordshire HR6 0QF
United Kingdom

(UK) ISBN-10: 0-85244-033-2
(UK) ISBN-13: 978-0-85244-033-9

FOREWORD

Saint Augustine's *Confessions* might well be described as one long heartfelt prayer culminating in the praise of the creative power of God the Father Almighty and the intrinsic order and beauty of all His creation. Augustine extols most especially the dignity of man wonderfully created in God's image and likeness, more wonderfully redeemed by Christ Jesus, thus enabling man to be sanctified by the Holy Spirit for the purpose of living eternal life on high in the blessed communion of the Most Holy Trinity, with all the Angels and Saints in light.

In the *Confessions*—commonly considered the first psychological autobiography—Saint Augustine commits himself to an inner spiritual search, which leads him to consider his conscience, dogma, and creation as *loci theologici* (theological sources) to develop the good habit of prayer. Augustine's are prayers of adoration, acknowledgement of God's manifold attributes, confession of and contrition for sin, thanksgiving, praise, and petition. Therefore, we have reason for great joy to discover, as Father Velocci's book explains from the outset, that in the nineteenth century, Newman's own unique experience of prayer from his childhood was steeped in the same sources and expressive of the same traditional types of prayer cherished by that fifth-century Doctor of the Church.

The parallels continue as we consider that Newman's conversion to Catholicism, forged in the crucible of hard prayer, work, study, and penitence, has been deemed the greatest since that of Augustine of Hippo. In fact, having studied Newman's own "confessions," his *Apologia pro Vita Sua*, scholars like Jean Guitton suggest that Newman was a Saint Augustine projected into our time.[1] Both Augustine and Newman held that prayer is one of the many evidences of God's existence, because it indicates that man by his very nature is not mere flesh and blood but also a cognitive creature, with memory, understanding and will, in possession of an immortal soul that makes him *capax Dei* (capable of God), as the *Catechism of the Catholic Church* teaches in its very first chapter.

Saint Thomas Aquinas composed such sublime Eucharistic hymns as the *O Salutaris* and *Tantum Ergo* while kneeling before the Blessed Sacrament. Newman, without being a Thomist himself, did combine faith and reason in his approach to divine worship, so much so, that the words of 1 Peter 3:15 spring to mind: "Always be prepared to make a defense to any one who calls you to account for the hope that is in you, yet do it with gentleness and reverence." Again, the sacred author of the Epistle to the Hebrews gives us a glimpse into the heart of Jesus' own prayer as the Incarnate Word when he writes: "In the days of his flesh Jesus offered up prayers and supplications, with loud cries and tears, to Him who was able to save Him from death, and He was heard for His godly fear" (5:7).

In this book the reader will find examples of prayers—such as Newman's beautiful translation of the *Anima Christi* and his meditation in the presence of the Blessed Sacrament—that express the reverential fear he manifested toward the Most Holy Eucharist, the great mystery of our faith, indeed its source and summit, as we have been taught by the Second Vatican Council.

[1] Cf. Jean Guitton, *Il Secolo Che Verrà*, trans. Antonietta Francavilla (Milan: Saggi Tascabili Bompiani, 1999), p. 144.

Mystical Doctors of the Church, including Teresa of Ávila, John of the Cross, and Thérèse of Lisieux, waxed eloquently on mental and vocal prayer, meditation, and contemplation of the divine mysteries.[2] These same areas of interest in Newman's life of prayer are emphasized throughout the present work.

Blessed Teresa of Calcutta[3] copied in her own hand a prayer book for the daily use of her Missionaries of Charity. In her handbook of prayers, one finds a cornucopia of traditional Catholic prayers and litanies such as those Newman himself used in his daily prayers and community life at the Oratory of Birmingham. As a matter of fact, Newman, having memorized whole sections of the Bible since his childhood, and influenced by the Caroline Divines of the seventeenth century, adapted or composed some biblically-based litanies for use during the various liturgical seasons. These litanies are very much akin to those found in the Anglican *Book of Common Prayer* and in the Divine Liturgies of Saints John Chrysostom and Basil the Great.[4]

Thus, Newman reminds us of the Latin adage *lex orandi, lex credendi* (the law of praying is the law of believing). Furthermore, Newman's prayers combine to

[2] One might consult the following classic works of mystical spirituality: St. Teresa of Ávila's *The Interior Castle* and *The Way of Perfection*; or *The Ascent of Mount Carmel*, *The Dark Night*, and *The Spiritual Canticle* of St. John of the Cross; or St. Thérèse's *Autobiography: Story of a Soul*.

[3] In the first encyclical of Pope Benedict XVI, *Deus Caritas Est* (God Is Love), we read: "In the example of Blessed Teresa of Calcutta we have a clear illustration of the fact that time devoted to God in prayer not only does not detract from effective and loving service to our neighbor but is in fact the inexhaustible source of that service. In her letter for Lent of 1996, Blessed Teresa wrote to her lay co-workers: 'We need this deep connection with God in our daily life. How can we obtain it? By prayer'" (no. 36).

[4] For these litanies and a veritable feast of Newman's prayers, the reader would do well to consult (and use personally!) the handsome and handy edition *Prayers, Verses and Devotions*, published by Ignatius Press.

form a synthesis of the noblest prayers found in various Christian traditions. We can dare to say that Newman was like the scribe lauded by Jesus in Matthew 13:51–52, for he had a knack for drawing forth the best of the old and the best of the new from the storeroom of the Church's collective experience of prayer throughout the centuries. Newman "breathed with both lungs," [5] by appreciating and appropriating prayer forms and methods of both the Eastern and Western churches. Consequently, a true ecumenist will find much that is useful in Newman's theology and spirituality of prayer to further the cause of Christian unity.

However, Newman accomplished all this without losing his remarkable English sensibility and Victorian style. Newman's devotionals, though pious, are not saccharine. He shied away from the mere sentimentalism and charismatic exuberance he associated with Italianate prayer, the type he had heard while visiting Naples and Sicily in June of 1833.

To trace the development of Newman's prayer, one would need to return to the Arcadian years Newman spent in the Oxford Movement as Vicar of Saint Mary's— Oxford University's parish church—and in his semi-monastic community at Littlemore. Eventually, Newman's faith and reason, supported by constant prayer, brought him to the conclusion that Anglicanism as the *Via Media* between Catholicism and Protestantism was, in his own words, "absolutely pulverized." Thus, Newman finally stood at the threshold of his conversion, which took place at Littlemore on October 9, 1845, through the ministration of an Italian Passionist missionary to England, Blessed Dominic Barberi of the Mother of God, who had

---

[5] "To breathe with both lungs," meaning to draw from the great liturgical, catechetical, and devotional patrimony of the Churches of East and West alike, was a favorite expression of Pope John Paul II.

set out from Oxford—on foot, through the pouring rain—
the previous night.[6]

Saint Alphonsus Liguori, one of Newman's admired
Catholic authors (and the founder of Father Velocci's religious family), is generally regarded as the Marian and
Eucharistic Doctor of the nineteenth century. It was he
who helped to inculcate in the Venerable Cardinal a
strong devotion to Mary under her various titles (e.g.,
Stella Maris, Star of the Sea) and to Our Lord's real and
abiding presence in the Most Holy Eucharist. Nevertheless, Newman's growth in devotion as regards Our
Blessed Lord and His holy Mother was nourished in no
small measure by the even earlier influence of John Keble
and Hurrell Froude.[7]

These men were two of Newman's dearest friends in
the Oxford Movement. Through their writings and devotional compositions,[8] they helped to water the seed of
Newman's faith, by which he would in due time come to
know Jesus through Mary (*Ad Iesum per Mariam*).[9] So
great was the Catholic Newman's devotion to the Virgin

[6] Every year, devotees of the Venerable Newman make a pilgrimage from
Oxford to Littlemore in remembrance of Blessed Dominic Barberi's first
pilgrimage begun on October 8, 1845. See *Friends of Cardinal Newman:
Newsletter* (The Oratory: Edgbaston, Birmingham, Christmas 2005), p. 16.

[7] In his *Apologia Pro Vita Sua*, Newman expressed his gratitude to and
admiration of Hurrell Froude, making special note of Froude's particular
devotion to the Blessed Virgin. Shortly before Newman's conversion to
Catholicism, he pays a personal tribute to John Keble and his Marian devotion in his *Essays Historical and Critical*, underscoring Keble's influence in
the Anglican Church and even more astonishingly his contribution to what
Newman terms "the revival of Catholicism," in Anglicanism.

[8] For example, John Keble, author of *The Christian Year*, wrote Marian
poetry, some of which was collected in a work entitled *Lyra Innocentium*
(The Lyre of the Innocent).

[9] The expression "To Jesus through Mary" is found in the writings of
Saint Louis Marie Grignon de Montfort. From Saint Louis de Montfort,
Pope John Paul II borrowed his motto, *Totus tuus* (Totally yours), referring
to the complete entrustment of his life to the Blessed Virgin Mary.

Mary that, when his eyesight failed him and he could no longer pray the Roman Breviary each day, he fingered his Rosary beads until his feeble fingers could not even handle the beads.

Newman's soul rapt in prayer, both in the ordinary and extraordinary[10] experiences of his long life, proved to be a most fertile soil for God's tilling, a ground made increasingly more fecund by the outpouring of the dew of the Holy Spirit with the passage of time.

Saint Josemaría Escrivá, the founder of *Opus Dei* (The Work of God), emphasized, as did Newman, the importance of praying constantly, following Saint Paul's exhortations in his epistles to pray in the all circumstances of our daily life.[11] I venture to say that Newman and Escrivá likewise drew inspiration for their prayer in part from Saint Benedict of Nursia, who considered the Sacred Liturgy the "work of God" par excellence. Newman and Escrivá epitomized in their own lives the Benedictine motto, *Ora et labora* (work and pray), which they accomplished most admirably *ad majorem Dei gloriam* (for the greater glory of God).[12]

---

[10] Perhaps the best-known prayer of Newman's is entitled "The Pillar of Cloud," commonly referred to by its first words, "Lead, Kindly Light." Newman composed this prayer during a strong storm that surged around the ship taking him back home to England from the Mediterranean. Newman was so sea-sick and afraid that he thought he was going to die.

[11] In a homily entitled "Towards Holiness," preached on November 26, 1967, Saint Josemaría Escrivá tells us: "We started out with the simple and attractive vocal prayers that we learned as children, prayers that we want never to abandon. Our prayer, which began so childlike and ingenuous, now opens out into a broad, smooth-flowing stream, for it follows the course of friendship with Him Who said: 'I am the Way.' If we so love Christ, if with divine daring we take refuge in the wound opened in His Side by the lance, then the Master's promise will find fulfillment: 'Whoever loves me, keeps my commandments, and my Father will love him and we will come to him and make our dwelling in him'" (*Friends of God*, no. 333).

[12] For a time, Newman wanted to become a Jesuit. St. Ignatius of Loyola used to joke about Philip Neri that he was like the bell of a church that

In this slim volume, Italian Redemptorist Father Giovanni Velocci, a renowned Newman scholar,[13] masterfully explores the several themes of Newman's theology of prayer. Father Velocci always has a clear view as to how Newman incorporated this theology into his daily spiritual life. The Italian title of his work, *La preghiera in Newman* (Prayer in Newman), has been mirrored in the title of this English edition because it is a clever pun that allows us to think of Newman and prayer as intrinsically intertwined. That is, this work opens up for us *prayer* as found in the corpus of Newman's writings, but equally the prayer that was *in Newman* the man.

Father Velocci's treatment of this subject is useful to both the Newman scholar and the Newman novice because he allows Newman to speak for himself, providing Newman's actual texts, and adding a helpful anthology of some of Newman's better-known prayers, meditations, and devotions.

Prayer, according to one of the ancient definitions found in the writings of the great Fathers and Doctors of the Church, is "the lifting up of the mind and heart to God." This is precisely the meaning found in the *Catechism of the Catholic Church*, no. 2559, citing an

---

called everybody into religious life while he, like the bell, remained outside. As a matter of fact, the members of the Oratory of St. Philip Neri are secular priests or lay brothers who do not profess the vows or evangelical counsels of poverty, chastity and obedience. Eventually, Newman decided to join the Congregation of the Oratory of St. Philip Neri, introducing the Oratory to England. In a homily entitled, "The Christian's Hope" (June 8, 1968), Saint Josemaría exhorted: "And do everything for God, thinking of His glory, with your sights set high and longing for the definitive homeland, because there is no other goal worthwhile" (*Friends of God*, no. 237).

[13] On a personal note, I should say that when I was doing research for my doctoral dissertation on Cardinal Newman's Mariology, Father Velocci very graciously gave of his time and insights to be of assistance to me. In some sense, then, I embarked on the present project as an act of gratitude to him for his kindness to me.

eighth-century Father of the Church, Saint John Damascene, whom Father Velocci also cites in these pages.

In other words, prayer, in its essence, as the Desert Fathers emphasized, is a *sacra conversatio* (sacred conversation) between the creature and the Creator. Newman would not only approve of this fundamental definition of prayer but would add that nothing—not even the sacred rites of the Church and the intercession of the Blessed Virgin Mary—can substitute for this personal, one-on-one relationship,[14] which the individual believer is called to maintain with the Persons of the Most Blessed Trinity through private prayer. Newman goes so far as to suggest that one who does not pray for himself first and foremost will never be effective in praying for others. Thus, Newman advocates, in a selfless Christian scheme of things, the old Latin saying: *primus vivere*—which is to say: take care of your own life of faith, your own salvation, before worrying about the spiritual life and salvation of others.

As Father Velocci explains, the Venerable Cardinal identified different types of prayer, as well as fundamental attitudes, or right dispositions of mind and spirit, that must accompany prayer, if it is to be efficacious or pleasing to God. Ultimately, Newman says, our prayer must conform itself as closely as possible to the prayer that we call perfect because it was taught by Our Lord to His disciples, namely, the Lord's Prayer or the Our Father.

Certainly, as Newman points out, prayer is a particular privilege and duty of the orthodox Christian believer, who participates through Baptism in the priestly, prophetic, and kingly offices of Christ. Newman underscores the vital necessity of prayer in the spiritual life of the

[14] In his *Essay on the Development of Christian Doctrine*, Newman refers to this relationship between the soul of the creature and his Creator as "*solus cum Solo*" (alone with the Alone).

believer when he says that prayer is to our spiritual life and well-being what our breathing and the beating of our pulse are to our physical life and well-being. Newman refers to intercessory prayer as the particular characteristic of the Christian.

Thus, at every turn, Cardinal Newman highlights the majestic place of prayer, the veritable core of all Christian doctrine and devotion. Prayer is so important that Newman makes one's eternal destiny hinge upon it. He states that prayer is the language of Heaven. Consequently, Newman explains that if a man here below is unaccustomed to prayer his whole life long, then how can he (or we) expect to see him (ourselves) immersed in it for all eternity? The only work of Heaven is unceasing prayer. By praying on earth, a human being already enters into that great chorus of prayer that the Angels conduct before the throne of God night and day.

For the Anglican Newman, but especially for Newman the convert to Catholicism, prayer entails not only the individual's pilgrimage of faith in his own "heart to heart"[15] conversation with God in his daily life but also his communal experience of the divine, which occurs through a devout participation in the sacramental life of the Church, the Mystical Body of Christ.

Newman, as Father Velocci helps us to see, is careful not to isolate private prayer from public or liturgical prayer. While Newman definitely keeps them distinct, he does not advocate an opposition or separation between the two. A person's private prayer should be fed from his daily hearing of the Word of God,[16] most especially in the context of the Eucharistic Sacrifice and in the

---

[15] "*Cor ad cor loquitur*" (Heart speaks to heart) was chosen by Newman for his cardinalatial motto. Newman took this motto because he admired its use in Saint Francis de Sales' *Introduction to the Devout Life*.

[16] Saint Paul teaches us in his Epistle to the Romans at 10:17 that "faith comes from hearing" the Word of God.

celebration of the other sacraments of faith and salvation. A person's private prayer should flow not merely from his own emotions in any particular time or place but should be linked to the enduring treasure of piety and devotion which the Saints have left us as our special inheritance in the Church.

Newman encourages us to strengthen the bond of our private prayer to that of the prayer offered up to God as a sweet-smelling oblation on the part of the entire communion of Saints, that great "cloud of witnesses" (Hebrews 12:1), who await the felicitous end of our journey toward God.[17]

It is likely that Cardinal Newman would also agree with the estimation of the French philosopher and mathematician Blaise Pascal, who remarked that the *desire* to prayer is itself a prayer. Before Newman discusses the various types of prayer, he posits in the human person a natural inclination or a God-given longing, a *desiderium Dei* (desire for God) such as Saint Augustine reflected on so often in his *Confessions*,[18] which propels him from within the very depths of his being to seek the face of the God of Abraham, Isaac, and Jacob, the God of Jesus Christ, and not merely the God of the Philosophers.

As Father Velocci also points out, prayer is, for Newman, the only sure means by which we can make sense out of our participation in the mystery of Our Lord's saving Incarnation and paschal dying and rising. Prayer, for Newman, is a passageway to the Sacred and Eucharistic Heart of Christ Jesus, in which we should find ourselves joined to the Immaculate Heart of Mary, His

[17] See Saint Bonaventure's *magnum opus* entitled *Itinerarium mentis in Deum* (The Journey of the Mind into God).

[18] Recall Saint Augustine's famous line from the *Confessions*: "*O Domine, quia tu fecisti nos et inquietum est cor nostrum donec requiescat in Te*" (O Lord, Thou hast made us for Thyself, and our heart is restless until it rests in Thee).

Mother and ours. This *cor ad cor loquitur*, this "heart to heart" sacred conversation between Divine Son and Mother, secures our own entrance in that abyss of God's own Heart, full of infinite love and mercy, which only the Spirit of God can scrutinize.

It is a tribute to Newman's manly virtue that we find in his writings several prayers dedicated to the honor of Saint Joseph, who was the foster-father and guardian of the Redeemer, the most chaste spouse of the Blessed Virgin Mary and loving patriarch of the Holy Family.

Newman exhorts us to follow the example of Our Blessed Lord and of Our Blessed Mother, and to a lesser degree the example of the other Saints, so that we might properly cultivate the virtues of humility, trust, perseverance, and purity of heart, without which no one can see God or even call upon Him to answer our prayers. With Newman, we must not forget that God answers or chooses not to answer our prayers according to His logic rather than our own. While we live in the confines of space and time, God lives in an eternal present, so that whenever in fact the Lord does answer our prayers, it is on His eternal watch and not according to the rhythms of our temporal timepiece.

Cardinal Newman was a man completely taken up with the notion of God's Providence. One could also safely say that Newman viewed prayer and all the earthly concerns that prayers are intended to envelope as existing *sub specie æternitatis* (from the perspective of eternity). He was convinced, and desired ever so fervently to convince us, that man proposes and God disposes. In simple terms, we need to learn to accept this reality, for it is just another sign of God's mysterious and providential love for each one of us.

In sum, then, we could say that Newman's theology of prayer reiterates the teaching of Saint Paul in Romans

8:26–27: "Likewise the Spirit helps us in our weakness; for we do not know how to pray as we ought, but the Spirit Himself intercedes for us with sighs too deep for words. And He who searches the hearts of men knows what is the mind of the Spirit, because the Spirit intercedes for the Saints according to the will of God."

It is my fervent hope that Father Velocci's book will be both educational and inspirational. I am confident that Cardinal Newman's own prayers and meditations can move anyone to pray well and often, perhaps even to sing well so as to pray twice, as Saint Augustine taught (*Qui cantat bene bis orat*).[19] May the Venerable Newman accompany us as we try to take another step each day "*ex umbris et imaginibus in veritatem*" (from shadows and images into the truth).[20] Let us seek his intercession and likewise pray that he will soon be raised to the honors of the altar.

Rev. Nicholas L. Gregoris, s.t.d.

FEBRUARY 21, 2006
205th anniversary of Newman's birth

---

[19] Like Saint Augustine, Newman was quite enamored of Gregorian/Ambrosian chant. Many of Newman's own poetic works have been set to beautiful and haunting melodies. For example, one thinks of how the composer Edgar Elgar superbly scored Newman's prolonged meditation on Purgatory, *The Dream of Gerontius*. Or, how Newman's hymn "Praise to the Holiest in the Heights" (likewise from *The Dream of Gerontius*) has become one of Christendom's cherished hymns, along with his prayer "Lead, Kindly Light."

[20] This was the epitaph he chose for his tombstone at Rednal.

ABBREVIATIONS

AP   *Apologia pro Vita Sua*
     (1864)

Dev.   *Essay on the Development of Christian Doctrine*
     (1845)

Diff.   *Certain Difficulties Felt by Anglicans in Catholic Teaching*
     (1850)

GA   *An Essay in Aid of a Grammar of Assent*
     (1870)

Idea   *Idea of a University*
     (1852)

MD   *Meditations and Devotions*
     (1881)

PPS   *Parochial and Plain Sermons*
     (1834–1843)

SN   *Sermon Notes*
     (1849–1878)

Var.   *Sermons Preached on Various Occasions*
     (1857)

SSD   *Sermons Bearing on Subjects of the Day*
     (1843)

NEWMAN AND PRAYER

In 1816, at the age of fifteen, John Henry Newman had an extraordinary religious experience, following which he felt himself united to God in a very intense way, which he described as *"making me rest in the thought of two and two only absolute and luminously self-evident beings, myself and my Creator"* (AP, 127). Such a union became stronger with the passage of time, absorbed him completely, and oriented his thought and action. It was a relationship of faith, based on the certainty of Christian revelation and on the love of God for him, and it manifested itself in constant and fervent prayer.

Prayer became the preferred occupation of Newman; it marked out all his days, assuming new aspects in successive phases of his life. Prayer accompanied him and comforted him during the period in which he was a student at Oxford; it became more frequent and open to others when he was appointed rector of the university church of St. Mary and tutor at Oriel College and in the years of crisis preceding his conversion to Catholicism. After his entrance into the Catholic Church in 1845, his prayer assumed another tone, enriched by a new dimension: It became simpler, more trusting, one could say more popular, expressing itself in practice and in the devout exercises of Catholic piety.

Newman did not keep such an important experience closed up within himself but made of it matter for reflection to comprehend it better and to bring it to the knowledge of others. In this development, he did not limit himself to reveal his personal sentiments, but enriched them with his study and the addition of what we could call the sources of his prayer: the Bible, the Tradition, the writings of the Caroline Divines,[1] the *Book of Common Prayer*. Newman often dealt with prayer in his writings and homilies, describing this prayer in all its aspects, although characterized by his own personality. These are the aspects of prayer we intend to present in this brief work.

Faith and Conscience—the Foundations of Prayer

Newman had a high estimation of prayer that for him constituted *"the very essence of all religion"* (Diff., 68), so much so as to cite with full approval, in this regard, the drastic phrase of his beloved Saint Philip Neri, that *"a man without prayer was an animal without reason"* (MD, 99). Using the example of the pagan Greeks and Romans, Newman noted that, even they, *"amid all their superstitions, were believers in an unseen Providence and in the moral law"*[2] and thus rendered their deities their due. He observed, presciently (already in the nineteenth century): *"But we are now coming to a time when the world does not acknowledge our first principles."*[3]

---

[1] The "Caroline Divines" were those Anglican preachers and theologians, from the time of Charles I and Charles II, who exhibited strong "Catholic" tendencies and hence were favored by members of the Oxford Movement.

[2] *Faith and Prejudice and Other Unpublished Sermons*, edited by Fathers of the Birmingham Oratory (New York: Sheed & Ward, 1956), p. 124.

[3] This entire sermon is, in fact, worth reading. It was delivered on October 2, 1873, for the opening of the first Catholic seminary in England since the Protestant Reformation, entitled "The Infidelity of the Future." In it, Cardinal Newman reflected on what the future priests would have to face: "My brethren, you are coming into a world, if present appearances do not deceive, such as priests never came into before, that is, so far forth as you do go into it, so far as you go beyond your flocks, and so far as those flocks may be in great danger as under the influence of the prevailing epidemic."

The rock-solid foundation of prayer for Newman, as for every believer, is faith. And faith, more properly speaking, is placed in a personal God. He says this himself by means of that most delicate personage known as Callista, in whom it seems that his bashfulness about spiritual confessions would have found an immediate outlet but so much more moving: *"I feel that God is within my heart. I feel myself in His presence. He says to me, 'Do this: don't do that.' You may tell me that this dictate is a mere law of my nature, as is to joy or to grieve. I cannot understand this. No, it is the echo of a person speaking to me. Nothing shall persuade me that it does not ultimately proceed from a person external to me. It carries with it its proof of its divine origin. My nature feels towards it as towards a person. When I obey it, I feel a satisfaction; when I disobey, a soreness—just like that which I feel in pleasing or offending some revered friend"* (*Callista*, 314).

The preceding text is very important, because to faith is joined, and almost made to coincide with it, the voice of conscience, of which Newman had always been a strenuous proponent. Nothing could be farther from the sentimental emotionalism and religious impressionism that made very clear and absolute sentiments of repulsion arise within Newman, even a bit too much so. In fact, notice how conscience is described by him: Every human being has within his spirit *"a certain commanding dictate,"* not a mere sentiment, not a simple opinion or impression or way of seeing things, but *"a law, an authoritative voice, bidding him do certain things and avoid others."* No one has power over this voice, or only with extreme difficulty; it was not man who created it, nor is it man who can destroy it. *"This is Conscience,"* declares Newman—and the upper case "C" is his; and its existence alone suggests to our mind the existence of a Being external to ourselves, *"else whence its strange, troublesome peremptoriousness?"* (Var., 64–65).

Conscience is such an anchor for Newman that he will one day write a very strong line: *"Were it not for this voice, speaking so clearly in my conscience and my heart, I should be an atheist, or a pantheist, or a polytheist when I looked into the world"* (AP, 334). Even though Newman experienced the anguish common to modern men and was also, but to a lesser degree, prone to the sense of the absurd and of the problematic that assails all of us, he had a source of strength which the modern world rarely remembers or is willing to use!

Dogma

It is faith based on conscience, that conscience which for Newman is the *"true inward guide"* (PPS I, 254) and of which he makes an unforgettable praise and, I would say, "portrait" in the sermon "The Self-Wise Inquirer" (214–225); it is faith, however, that has another and not less firm support, another element and proof of absolute certitude: dogma.

What *"the dogmatic principle in the history of Christianity"* (Dev., 361) was, writes Newman (highlighting the parallelism between these two guarantees of our faith), so *"conscience is in the history of an individual soul"* (361). But also speaking of his *"individual soul,"* he was able to say: *"When I was fifteen, (in the autumn of 1816), a great change of thought took place in me. I fell under the influences of a definite Creed, and received into my intellect impressions of dogma, which, through God's mercy, have never been effaced or obscured"* (AP, 107). And he repeats: *"From the age of fifteen, dogma has been the fundamental principle of my religion: I know no other religion; I cannot enter into the idea of any other sort of religion; religion, as a mere sentiment, is to me a dream and a mockery"* (AP, 150).

Exiting from his autobiographical confession, New-

man can affirm: *"But the very idea of Christianity in its pro-
fession and history, is something more than this; it is a
'Revelatio revelata;' it is a definite message from God to man
distinctly conveyed by His chosen instruments, and to be received as such a message; and therefore to be positively acknowledged, embraced, and maintained as true, on the ground
of its being divine, not as true on intrinsic grounds, not as
probably true, or partially true, but as absolutely certain knowledge, certain in a sense in which nothing else can be certain,
because it comes from Him Who neither can deceive nor be
deceived"* (GA, 386–387).

Prayer—Duty and Privilege

One could put together a little anthology (and a most
beautiful and useful one) by gathering together what
Newman has written on these essential points: faith in a
personal God, conscience, dogma. But we believe that
what we have presented is enough for our purpose to
demonstrate how faith in a personal God, guaranteed by
conscience and dogma, justifies and even demands as a
necessary duty the humble service of prayer. With good
reason, Newman considers external prayer and interior
prayer, that is to say, every form of prayer, as *"natural duties,"* even prescindng from Christian Revelation. *"These
two types of praying are also natural duties. I mean, we should
in a way be bound to attend to them, even if we were born in a
heathen country and had never heard of the Bible. For our conscience and reason would lead us to practice them, if we did but
attend to these divinely-given informants"* (PPS VII, 204).

Not only that, but as the dictates of conscience are
confirmed by the revelations of dogma, likewise is the
natural desire for prayer reinforced by the express command to pray given to us by Jesus, so much so, that
Newman highly praises those who *"when He [Jesus] says*

'Pray,' 'Continue in prayer,' take His words simply, and forthwith Pray, and that instantly" (PPS III, 317). In great detail, Newman explains to us how the Sacred Scriptures establish prayer as an absolute and inescapable duty (see PPS VII, 207ff.).

That prayer would be a duty, is one of the truths the author repeated frequently and with great conviction. Often, to the idea of duty is joined that of *privilege*; to unite the two concepts in a single formula, we recall the sentence: *"Prayer, praise, thanksgiving, contemplation, are the peculiar privilege and duty of a Christian . . ."* (PPS IV, 227). There we see already how Newman intends prayer in all its forms, from intercession, that seems always to be implied in the initial end of prayer, to contemplation.

The Definition of Prayer

At this point, having established that prayer is a rational duty and an explicit order of Sacred Scripture, we could ask ourselves for a *definition of prayer*. Just as Newman was moved up to now according to the well-traveled ways of Christian doctrine, so now we find him perfectly aligned with the most secure biblical, patristic and catechetical tradition of Catholicism (and, one should mind well that up until this point Newman is still an Anglican).

"What is prayer? Newman asks. And he responds: *"It is (if it may be said reverently) conversing with God"* (PPS IV, 227). From here he passes on to praise this *"conversing with God,"* culminating with the assertion: *"I say then, it is plain to common sense that the man who has not accustomed himself to the language of Heaven will be no fit inhabitant of it when, in the Last Day, it is perceptibly revealed"* (229). Is this not in perfect harmony with St. Gregory of Nyssa's *"oratio conversatio sermoncinatioque cum Deo est"* (prayer is a conversation and discussion with God)?

We are familiar with the famous patristic definition of prayer as the *"ascensus mentis in Deum"* (the raising of the mind toward God) of Saint John Damascene, as well as the *"mentis ad Deum affectuosa intentio"* (the affectionate intention of the mind toward God) of Saint Augustine; Newman springs up with phrases that are a modern paraphrase of them. Therefore, we limit ourselves to that passage in which he affirms it to be the duty and privilege of all disciples of the Lord to *". . . live in Heaven in their thoughts, motives, aims, desires, likings, prayers, praises, intercessions, even while they are in the flesh; to look like other men, to be busy like other men, to be passed over in the crowd of men, or even to be scorned or oppressed, as other men may be, but the while to have a secret channel of communication with the Most High, a gift the world knows not of; to have their life hid with Christ in God"* (PPS VI, 214)—which is the most beautiful way of defining prayer in its highest and most disinterested manifestations.

Then we have the other classical definition of prayer as the *"petitio decentium a Deo"* (the prayer of the decent ones to God), once again belonging to Saint John Damascene; this definition, however, is more restricted and concerns only one type of prayer. Aside from numerous interventions, Newman dedicated an entire sermon to this specific theme, entitled "Intercession" (PPS III, 350–366); we will treat this later on.

Adoration

We now come to a more particular examination of prayer, that prayer which is a *"characteristic of Christians"* (SSD, 280), which the New Testament describes, and which must always exist. We recall that according to its purpose, we distinguish between *adoration* and *petition*.

All the works of Newman are full of adoration—so

much so, that one has an embarrassing array of choice in this regard. Therefore, rather than choosing some phrases in which Newman inculcates the obvious primacy of adoration of God, we prefer to provide an example of one of his prayers of adoration, for that is always not only the best way to glean his ideas, but the particular way with which his ineffable personality realizes it and puts it into practice. Let us listen to him:

"My Lord, I believe, and know, and feel, that Thou art the Supreme Good. And, in saying so, I mean, not only supreme Goodness and Benevolence, but that Thou art the sovereign and transcendent Beautifulness. I believe that, beautiful as is Thy creation, it is mere dust and ashes, and of no account, compared with Thee, Who art the infinitely more beautiful Creator. I know well, that therefore it is that the Angels and Saints have such perfect bliss, because they see Thee. To see even the glimpse of Thy true glory, even in this world throws holy men into an ecstasy. And I feel the truth of all this, in my own degree, because Thou hast mercifully taken our nature upon Thee, and hast come to me as man. 'Et vidimus gloriam ejus, gloriam quasi Unigeniti a Patre'—'and we saw His glory, the glory as it were of the only begotten of the Father.' The more, O my dear Lord, I meditate on Thy words, works, actions, and sufferings in the Gospel, the more wonderfully glorious and beautiful I see Thee to be" (MD, 331).

Anyone who knows how to compose a prayer like that is undoubtedly a master of adoration. Furthermore, Newman affirms that *"worship and service make up their [the Angels'] blessedness; and such is our blessedness in proportion as we approach them"* (PPS VIII, 265). Newman always fought the prejudice according to which religion would consist only in benefiting one's neighbor: *". . . how different is the spirit of this [Christ's] prayer! Evil round about Him, enemies and persecutors in His path, temptation in prospect, help for the day, sin to be expiated, God's will in His heart, God's*

Name on His lips, God's Kingdom in His hopes: this is the view it gives us of a Christian" (SSD, 289).

Praise and Thanksgiving

Closely united to adoration are praise and thanksgiving, as we have already seen affirmed by Newman and as every Catholic catechism unanimously establishes: *"[W]e should follow David and Jacob, by living in constant praise and thanksgiving..."* (PPS V, 83). By chance we gather, among the myriad praises to his God, this little most illuminating sketch: *"My God, I believe and know and adore Thee as infinite in the multiplicity and depth of Thy attributes. I adore Thee as containing in Thee an abundance of all that can delight and satisfy the soul"* (MD, 432).

As for thanksgiving, Newman recommends: *"Well were it for us, if we had the character of mind instanced in Jacob, and enjoined on his descendants: the temper of dependence upon God's Providence, and thankfulness under it, and careful memory of all He has done for us"* (PPS V, 82).

We find a concrete example of this in Newman's diary on June 25, 1869, where he declares how marvelous the Providence of God has been to him throughout his whole life; and where, after having noted that even adversities have ended up by serving him well, he concludes: *"Among the ordinary mass of men,* no one *has sinned so much,* no one *has been so mercifully treated, as I have;* no one *such cause for humiliation, such cause for thanksgiving."* [4]

Reparation

Already in the previous citation, together with the recognition of the good things received from God, we discover

---

[4] Found in *John Henry Newman: Autobiographical Writings*, edited with an Introduction by Henry Tristam of the Oratory (New York: Sheed & Ward, 1955), p. 268.

the element of *reparation*, of *expiation* that proceeds from a sincere *confession* of one's own faults *("no one has sinned so much")*, as well as sincere *contrition ("no one such cause for humiliation")*. Newman will never be deaf to this part of the Christian creed and this aspect of prayer.

Let us listen to but a part of Newman's meditation on sin: *"O my God, I am utterly confounded to think of the state in which I lie! What is my life, O my dear and merciful Lord, but a series of offences, little or great, against Thee! O what great sins I have committed against Thee before now—and how continually in lesser matters I am sinning! My God, what will become of me? What will be my position hereafter if I am left to myself! What can I do but come humbly to Him Whom I have so heavily affronted and insulted, and beg Him to forgive the debt which lies against me? O my Lord Jesus, Whose love for me has been so great as to bring Thee down from Heaven to save me, teach me, dear Lord, my sin—teach me its heinousness— teach me truly to repent of it—and pardon it in Thy great mercy!"* (MD, 336).

Petition

After adoration, an end or goal of prayer can be that of *petition*. It is only deplorable that for many this is the sole form of prayer, while they forget completely or largely adoration, which we have just highlighted. Newman, as we have already seen, gives adoration, praise, thanksgiving and reparation their due. But, afterwards, in his balanced Christian realism, he does not overlook by any means the prayer of petition; on the contrary, he studies and recommends it with insistence, frequency, and rare lucidity.

In his mature period, Newman wrote a prayer in which he asked precisely for the gift because the efficaciousness and value of intercession are so great. Let us take a look at this prayer: *"O my Lord Jesu, I will use the time. It will be too late to pray, when life is over. There is no prayer in the grave—there is no meriting in Purgatory. Low as I am in Thy all-holy sight, I am strong in Thee, strong through Thy Immaculate Mother, through Thy Saints: and thus I can do much for the Church, for the world, for all I love. O let me not walk my own way without thinking of Thee. Let me bring every-thing before Thee, asking Thy leave for everything I purpose, Thy blessing on everything I do . . ."*.[5] And he continues: *"It [the world] has no experience of the operations of grace, of the efficacy of the Sacraments, of the power of prayer . . ."* (Var., 195).

Newman was perfectly aware of the power of prayer, and, as we said, he dedicated a sermon to this theme, entitled "Intercession." That work may be as powerful as the famous treatise of Saint Alphonsus Liguori, entitled, "*Del gran mezzo della preghiera*" [Concerning the Great Means of Prayer].

Let us give a brief sketch of this sermon, at least for the purpose of giving examples of the contents of New-man's entire treatise dedicated to this topic of interest to us.

Newman takes as a motto a phrase of Saint Paul: "Pray at all times in the Spirit, with all prayer and suppli-cation. To that end keep alert with all perseverance, mak-ing supplication for all the saints" (Ephesians 6:18).

From the beginning, after affirming that *"prayer for self is the most obvious of duties"* (PPS III, 350), Newman im-mediately places next to it, as warmly recommended by the apostles, *"prayer for others."* Then Newman makes that more specific as prayer *"for ourselves with others, for the Church, and for the world, that it may be brought into the Church"* (ibid.).

[5] Wilfrid Ward, *The Life of John Henry Cardinal Newman* (London: Long-mans & Green, 1912), vol. II, 365.

"Intercession," as defined by Newman at this point, *"is the characteristic of Christian worship, the privilege of the heavenly adoption, the exercise of the perfect and spiritual mind"* (PPS III, 350–351). After that, Newman goes on to affirm, on the basis of numerous citations from the New Testament, how much intercession for others was recommended and practiced in the first and exemplary apostolic era (although without denying the legitimacy and nobility of prayer for oneself). Newman himself gives the reason for this when he writes: *"Nor could it be otherwise, if Christianity be a social religion, as it is pre-eminently. If Christians are to live together, they will pray together; and united prayer is necessarily of an intercessory character, as being offered for each other and for the whole. In proportion, then, as unity is an especial Gospel-duty, so does Gospel-prayer partake of a social character; and intercession becomes a token of the existence of a Church Catholic"* (352–353).

And so, following a trail of New Testament examples, Newman goes on immediately to demonstrate that *"intercession is the kind of prayer distinguishing a Christian from such as are not Christians"* (PPS III, 353). In fact, one not yet in the grace of God, one not yet a Christian cannot intercede for others, he would hold: *"We need not, I say, go to Scripture for information on so plain a point. Our first prayers must be for ourselves. Our own salvation is our personal concern; till we labour to secure it, till we try to live religiously, and pray to be enabled to do so, nay, and have made progress, it is but hypocrisy, or at best it is overbold, to busy ourselves with others"* (354).

However, he also admits: *"Nor would I deny, that a care for the souls of other men may be the first symptom of a man's beginning to think about his own . . ."* (PPS III, 355), but, in general, fallen man must begin—and begins effectively— by praying for himself.

But will God hear us? Certainly not sinners, says

Newman, who in this respect seems much more rigorous than many of the Saints. What about those who are not sinners? The Scriptures seem to assure us that God does not know how to resist the prayer of one who *"add[s] to our faith virtue"* (PPS III, 356). Immediately afterwards, he makes this truth more precise: *"[I]t is a caution to us, who rightly insist on the prerogatives imparted by His grace, ever to remember that it is grace only that ennobles and exalts us in His sight. Abraham is our spiritual father; and as he is, so are his children. In us, as in him, faith must be the foundation of all that is acceptable with God"* (359). For Newman still an Anglican as for the Council of Trent, faith was the *radix justificationis* ["the root of justification"]: *"The very instinct of faith will lead a man to do this without set command, and the Sacraments secure its observance"*(ibid.).

But notice once again the perfect equilibrium of Newman, that we have called his classical spirituality. Immediately after this exaltation of faith, Newman hastens to make this more precise: *"So much then, by way of caution, on the influence of faith upon our salvation, furthering it, yet not interfering with the distinct office of works in giving virtue to our intercession"* (PPS III, 359).

With a certain subtlety more appropriate to an exegetical essay than to a parochial sermon, our author proceeds to explain: *"It is then by a similar appointment that intercession is the prerogative and gift of the obedient and holy"* (PPS III, 361). And here Newman exalts intercession to the highest level, making us consider that Jesus, *". . . died to bestow upon him [the Christian] that privilege which implies or involves all others, and brings him into nearest resemblance to Himself, the privilege of intercession"* (362). Having recognized man's misery, he also points to his excellence, thanks to the gifts and merits of Christ, concluding that the Christian *"is made after the pattern and in the fullness of Christ—he is what Christ is. Christ intercedes above, and he intercedes below"* (363).

At this point, Newman sings one of the most beautiful hymns that has ever been lifted up in prayer, and in particular as a prayer of intercession, concerning which Newman underscores the divine dignity, the unimaginable power, that makes of the sinner a friend, a confidant of God, capable of encompassing the great events of the universe and of influencing their course in the presence of the Lord of all things.[6]

Do we doubt that it would be granted us, on account of our dignity, to make use of such a gift? Newman is explicit: *"The privilege of intercession is a trust committed to all Christians who have a clear conscience and are in full communion with the Church. We leave secret things to God—what each man's real advancement is in holy things, and what his real power in the unseen world. Two things alone concern us, to exercise our gift and make ourselves more and more worthy of it"* (PPS III, 364).

The text that follows is stupendous, even from an artistic standpoint:

"By words and works we can but teach or influence a few; by our prayers we may benefit the whole world, and every individual of it, high and low, friend, stranger, and enemy. Is it not fearful then to look back on our past lives in this one respect? How can we tell but that our king, our country, our Church, our institutions, and our own respective circles, would be in far happier circumstances than they are, had we been in the practice of more earnest and serious prayer for them" (PPS III, 365).

Finally comes an exhortation to be as God wants us to be, and the marvelous sermon concludes.[7]

---

[6] There are two pages (363–364) I would like to present in their entirety, but that would exceed the limits of our present research.—G. V.

[7] See PPS III, 365–366.

As one can see, the various forms of prayers of petition are all contemplated, and with their more true and sublime justifications of faith, reason, and divine command. Newman puts into a proper light that primary petition which is prayer for oneself, but above all intercession for others, and in a most particular way communal prayer, of which one finds such beautiful examples in the Early Church.

It is not necessary to bring forth other examples to show that our author intends this prayer of intercession for every class of the living (*". . . by our prayers we may benefit the whole world, and every individual of it, high and low, friend, stranger, and enemy"*); and as for intercession for the deceased, why not go in one's mind to the "Prayer for the Faithful Departed," composed by Newman himself, a most tender imploring of *"Jesu, Lover of souls"* (MD, 205), that He might grant pardon and eternal peace to all who have sinned in this life: *"Let their souls rejoice in Thy light, and impute not to them their former iniquities, which they committed through the violence of passion, or the corrupt habits of their fallen nature"* (ibid.). This intercession is strengthened by the invocation of a goodly number of Angels and Saints.

Vocal Prayer and Mental Prayer

Having seen what the goals of prayer are, we must yet say something about its forms. Prayer is distinguished first and foremost, with regard to its mode of expression, as vocal and mental prayer. Newman himself makes this distinction: *"There are two modes of praying mentioned in Scripture; the one is prayer at set times and places, and in set forms; the other is what the text speaks of,—continual or habitual prayer. The former of these is what is commonly called prayer, whether it be public or private. The other kind of praying may also be called holding communion with God, or living in God's sight . . ."* (PPS VII, 204).

We have just seen how the author, although praying from an intense interior life, never disparaged, but rather practiced vocal prayer even to the point of expressing a moving sincerity about it. Nor could a lover of the Rosary and of the Divine Office like Newman have overlooked or held in little account the adoration man gives to God not only with his mind, but also with his lips, tongue, and voice. As for mental prayer, we believe that few in the nineteenth century knew, studied, recommended, and appreciated it more than Newman—or only as Newman did.

One of Newman's most beautiful sermons, preached while still an Anglican, is dedicated to "Mental Prayer" or "Interior Prayer"; and since Newman is magisterial on this topic, we will give an overview of it. Newman begins with the distinction between prayer and mental prayer, and then passes on to demonstrate that it is a natural duty, even apart from biblical commands, to pray without ceasing.

"A man cannot really be religious one hour, and not religious the next. We might as well say he could be in a state of good health one hour, and in bad health the next. A man who is religious, is religious morning, noon, and night . . ." (PPS VII, 205). Everything, in a religious person, converges in prayer, so that in all things one sees the will of God. *"And a person who does this may be said almost literally to pray without ceasing."* Moreover, *"to be religious is, in other words, to have the habit of prayer, or to pray always"* (206). Is it difficult to achieve such an ideal?

Unfortunately, yes, but we have a living example in Christ, Who *"lived in the perfection of unceasing prayer"* (PPS VII, 207). If this is valid according to natural logic, it is even more so the case according to the Word of God, for Sacred Scripture expressly commands it for us. In fact, we see how miserable and fallible man would be, the prey of sin and damnation, if God, through the Holy Spirit, had not planted within us a new spiritual life, the so-called life of the soul. This mysterious life, of which we are certain but of which we are able to say so little, nonetheless still contains all our richness, all our hope.

We have within us the presence of the Holy Spirit: *"But as our bodily life discovers itself by its activity, so is the presence of the Holy Spirit in us discovered by a spiritual activity; and this activity is the spirit of continual prayer. Prayer is to spiritual life what the beating of the pulse and the drawing of the breath are to the life of the body"* (PPS VII, 209).

Where does Scripture say this? Everywhere the Scriptures tell us about the relationship between our spiritual rebirth and faith, *". . . for what is prayer but the expression, the voice, of faith?"* (PPS VII, 209). It is faith, in fact, that keeps us in continual conversation with God, to Whom go always our thoughts and affection: *"We begin to see God in all things by faith, and hold continual intercourse with Him by prayer. . . ."* He continues: *"Thus the true Christian pierces through the veil of this world and sees the next. He holds intercourse with it; he addresses God, as a child might address his parent, with as clear a view of Him; with deep reverence indeed, and godly fear and awe, but still with certainty and exactness . . ."* (210).

Unfortunately, Newman must conclude that, in general, we do not know how to pray: we are ungrateful, distracted, disordered, or we entrust ourselves to an *"accidental excitement, which is no test of a religious heart"* (PPS VII, 212). The reason is the smallness of our faith which does not allow us to see the invisible world with the eyes of the spirit. It is not a question of saying many words, for they are harmful to true prayer. What is important is to keep ourselves continually before the face of God. On this point, with great severity, Newman makes us think about what will become of us when, on the day of final reckoning, we shall find ourselves recorded in the book of God, not as having offered holy and continuous prayers, but as having offered frivolous and impious ones without end. On that day, we shall judge as wise those who today seem to be too spiritual and too austere, and we shall be sorry for not having practiced here on earth that unceasing prayer we scorned when it was inculcated in us and recommended to us. If we were to realize that Satan continuously seeks to distract us in our prayer to God, we would be so shocked at that realization as to tremble from fear. Let us seek to avoid such a ruination, remembering that *"they who ever speak with God in their hearts, are in turn taught by Him in all knowledge; but they who refuse to act upon the light, which God gave them by nature, at length come to lose it altogether, and are given up to a reprobate mind"* (215–216).

Meditation

As for meditation, which is the food of mental prayer, we know how Newman would have practiced it throughout his entire life, even if going against his inclinations and overcoming strong difficulties, precisely doing so because he considered it necessary.

Meditations and Devotions contains marvelous examples of meditations, particularly his "Meditations on Christian Doctrine,"[8] which derive their motivation for spiritual reflection from acts of contrition, from good resolutions, and from the illumination of the mind and the heart from the entire Catholic creed.

Two subjects particularly dear to Newman, however,

[8] MD, 213–346.

are Jesus and His Passion. Still an Anglican, Newman wrote: *"You will ask, how are we to learn to feel pain and anguish at the thought of Christ's sufferings? I answer, by thinking of them, that is, by dwelling on them"* (PPS VII, 135).

And besides: *"What is meditating on Christ? It is simply this, thinking habitually and constantly of Him and of His deeds and sufferings. It is to have Him before our minds as One Whom we may contemplate, worship, and address when we rise up, when we lie down, when we eat and drink, when we are at home and abroad, when we are working, or walking, or at rest, when we are alone, and again when we are in company; this is meditating"* (PPS VI, 41).

The other subject of meditation that Newman preferred was Mary, to whom he dedicated his exquisite *Meditations for the Month of May*.[9]

A concrete example of Newman's meditation is afforded us from the following plan that he traced out for the feast of All Saints:

1. *Place yourself in the presence of God, kneeling with hands clasped.*
2. *Read slowly and devoutly, Apocalypse, vii. 9–17.*
3. *Bring all this before you as in a picture.*
4. *Then say to Him whatever comes into your mind to say; for instance—*

   "They are before the throne of God, and serve Him day and night in His Temple." "They shall not hunger nor thirst any more"; "The Lamb shall lead them to the fountains of living waters."

   (1) My dear Lord and Saviour, shall I ever see Thee in Heaven? This world is very beautiful, very attractive, and there are many things and persons whom I love in it. But

[9] See MD, 1–77.

Thou art the most beautiful and best of all. Make me acknowledge this with all my heart, as well as by faith and in my reason.

(2) My Lord, I know nothing here below lasts; nothing here below satisfies. Pleasures come and go; I quench my thirst and am thirsty again. But the Saints in Heaven are always gazing on Thee, and drinking in eternal blessedness from Thy dear and gracious and most awful and most glorious countenance.

5. Conclusion. May my lot be with the Saints. [10]

As can be seen, this is a page of unmistakable Newmanian sensibility fallen into a perfectly Ignatian scheme.

Contemplation

Mental prayer and meditation, if practiced well, necessarily lead to *contemplation*. On this subject of the contemplative life, Newman has left us an entire sermon, "The Good Part of Mary," a clear allusion in the title, to that "better part" that, according to Jesus, was chosen by the sister of Martha and which "shall not be taken from her"; in that conversation with Jesus, we discover the essentials of the contemplative life.

In this sermon, after having recalled the words of Jesus in order to make a fundamental distinction between active service and contemplation, Newman lists various categories that appear singularly adapted to this second type of piety: the old, priests, especially if they are elderly, children, celibates, but in a particular way the blessed souls in the after-life. The "part of Mary" has always been held in high esteem in the Church, and various texts from the apostolic era confirm that.

[10] Ward, II, 366–367.

During the persecutions, the contemplative life was often impeded, but taken up again every time it became possible, even if always the heritage of but a few.

The times of Newman, according to Newman's own judgment, were not very favorable to contemplation. The modern world likewise despises Martha, that is, the active service of God, and if it appreciates it at all, it would be in terms of quantity, rather than quality. Therefore, *"Blessed indeed are they whom Christ calls near to Him to be His own peculiar attendants and familiar friends; more blessed if they obey and fulfill their calling! Blessed even if they are allowed to seize intervals of such service towards Him; but favoured and honoured beyond thought, if they can, without breach of duty, put aside worldly things with full purpose of heart, renounce the pursuit of wealth, keep clear of family cares, and present themselves as a holy offering, without spot or blemish, to Him Who died for them"* (PPS IV, 333–334).

Private Prayer: Forms and Times

Another distinction of prayer, as to its form, is that between *private* and *public* prayer, a distinction very much present to the spirit of Newman. As for private prayer, our Newman dedicated two sermons, "Forms of Private Prayer"[11] and "Times of Private Prayer."[12] The first sermon is marked by a healthy suspicion with regard to every form that, entrusted solely to our religious subjectivity, inevitably would fall into the risk of irreverence in addressing the Supreme Maker, or would get lost in *"their own thoughts at random"* that do not make for true piety, or that would exalt itself in *"using words that come into their minds,"* that exchanges our psychological and sensual

[11] PPS I, 257–270.
[12] PPS I, 244–256.

exaltation for the conversation owed to God. Newman asserts that there are *"these two undeniable truths, first, that all men have the same spiritual wants, and, secondly, that they cannot of themselves express them"* (PPS I, 258). Not for nothing, then, does Newman cite at the beginning of the sermon, the request posed to Jesus by the disciples: "Lord, teach us to pray" (Lk 11:1).

Therefore, one needs to pray according to a plan, in such a manner as to do it properly even when we do not feel inside ourselves any sensible fervor, or when memory abandons us, transforming prayer into a truly habitual act that could help us in the face of worldly distractions and from falling into sin again. To return to the origins, here as elsewhere, is the most secure watch-word: at the origins of our faith as children (*". . . what friends do they seem to find amid their gloom in the words they learned in their boyhood,—a kindly voice, aiding them to say what they otherwise would not know how to say . . ."* [PPS I, 267]), but above all at the origins of the Church, where the same Jesus teaches us, in the *Pater Noster*, the prayer that the apostles and all the Saints would have subsequently recited. *"Thus does the Lord's Prayer bring us near to Christ, and to His disciples in every age. . . . Nor can we use it too often; it contains in itself a sort of plea for Christ's listening to us . . ."* (269).

The sermon ends with the same warning against sentimentalism and cheap talk: *"The works of every day, these are the tests of our glorious contemplations, whether or not they shall be available to our salvation; and he who does one deed of obedience for Christ's sake, let him have no imagination and no fine feeling, is a better man, and returns to his home justified rather than the most eloquent speaker, and the most sensitive hearer, of the glory of the Gospel, if such men do not practice up to their knowledge"* (PPS I, 270).

Some concepts are repeated in the sermon about

Times of Private Prayer. God blesses the one who prays well, for he needs to make the most of it, because prayer is not only *"the unspeakable privilege"* (PPS I, 245), but also a precise duty of the Christian. Once again Newman reminds us: *" . . . we know well enough that we are bound to be in one sense in prayer and meditation all the day long"* (246). Now, it is obvious that public worship requires precise times, but the same holds for private worship, even if with more flexibility, for it must not be totally left to itself and to our fancy.

"Even our Saviour had His peculiar seasons of communing with God" (PPS I, 246), and the New Testament is full of examples and recommendations about the regularity and the periodic nature of prayer and of the acts of worship. Among the advantages of this practice, are that *"it brings religious subjects before the mind in regular course"* (248) and that *". . . it is also a more direct means of gaining from God an answer to our requests"* (269). How can one relinquish this great privilege of being able *"to move God"* (250), obtaining everything from Him through faith, of which, as we have already said, prayer is the voice? Beyond everything else, prayer at fixed hours calms the spirit, and *"stated times of prayer put us in that posture (as I may call it) in which we ought ever to be . . ."* (249). Therefore, we must resist our natural reluctance to pray at fixed hours; in a dramatic tone, Newman predicts ruinous consequences: *"When you have given over the practice of stated prayer, you gradually become weaker without knowing it"* (254). One should always recall that *"[Satan] perceives well enough that stated private prayer is the very emblem and safeguard of true devotion to God. . . . He who gives up regularity in prayer has lost a principal means of reminding himself that spiritual life is obedience to a Lawgiver, not a mere feeling or a taste"* (253), *". . . whereas, he who is strict in the observance of prayer morning and evening, praying with his heart as well as his lips,*

can hardly go astray, for every morning and evening brings him a monitor to draw him back and restore him" (255).

Public Prayer

Therefore, that which regards *public* prayer, public worship, is noted a great deal by Newman, during his entire life, both as an Anglican and as a Catholic, and it was used in the sense of making the Liturgy one of his most vivid meditations, preoccupations, and necessities. Already the house of God seemed to him the symbol of a higher reality. *"The very disposition of the building, the subdued light, the aisles, the Altar, with its pious adornments, are figures of things unseen, and stimulate our fainting faith"* (PPS III, 251). For this reason, the celebration of Sunday is so important, *"and if such is the effect of coming to Church once a week, even to an undecided or carnal mind, how much more impressive and invigorating are the Services to serious men who come daily or frequently!"* (251–252).

Newman's sense of urgency about attendance at public or community prayer causes him to pen a sermon entitled, "The Daily Service."[13] Always attentive to the origins of things, Newman begins by presenting daily worship as a common fact of apostolic times. Here one is not dealing with a time-conditioned precept, suitable for those times only, but a perennial precept, thus also meant for our times, indeed more urgent and needed today than ever, given so many certain modern errors. In particular, he highlights the popularity of *"a rational faith, so called, and a religion of the heart"* (PPS III, 304), which demonstrate the need for such prayer. Consulting the apostles, we find numerous and authoritative examples of prayer in common celebrated at a fixed hour and without interrup-

[13] PPS III, 301–317.

tion, considered precisely as a duty: *"Thus in the Lord's Prayer itself there seems to be sanction for daily united prayer"* (306).

As a good Anglican, Newman finds confirmation for his thesis in the prescriptions, fallen into disuse, found in the *Book of Common Prayer*; that source inspires him to decide to restore the daily service in his parish of Saint Mary.

According to Newman, those present might not be many (a foresight unfortunately verified in the reality), but that is not important. However, those absent will be able to participate in spirit in the acts of worship held in church in their name: what counts is not the number of faithful gathered in a temple, but our association with the intentions of Christ, the praying priest: *"So I account a few met together in prayer to be a type of His true Church . . ."* (PPS III, 314).

In two inspired pages, Newman shows us a picture of this Church made up of souls in prayer, where one feels the presence of the Angels, in a mutual union that the world does not know how to give. This is a consoling and joyful vision, but this should not cause us to marvel since *"it is in the nature of things that Christ's word must be a law* while *it is good tidings"* (PPS III,317).

The Effects of Prayer

We have seen the definition of prayer, the various types of prayer as to their purpose and forms. At this point it remains for us to ask ourselves what would be, according to Newman, the *effects* of prayer. Also here, every Roman catechism, or the most cited treatise of Saint Alphonsus Liguori, are in perfect harmony with the English spiritual master, whether one considers Newman before or after his conversion to the Church of Rome.

Among the many effects attributed to prayer in the vast *corpus* of Newman's work, we choose only some. For example, as all the Saints of one accord maintain and with support for the rest on precise biblical witnesses, prayer is a formidable instrument for the purpose of subjecting our passions. This time, we have an entire sermon dedicated to the topic in "Religious Worship a Remedy for Excitements."[14]

Newman begins by defining prayer and praise as a *"universal remedy, a panacea"* (PPS III, 336) for all our passions. We are unfortunately in the grasp of a thousand mundane agitations, a thousand distractions and worse: however, public worship is a marvelous source of equilibrium for one's spirit: *"What kinder office is there, when a man is agitated, than for a friend to put his hand upon him by way of warning, to startle and recall him? It often has the effect of saving us from angry words, or extravagant talking, or inconsiderate jesting, or rash resolves. And such is the blessed effect of the sacred Services on Christians busied about many things; reminding them of the one thing needful, and keeping them from being drawn into the great whirlpool or time and sense"* (339–340). This is an effect brought about in a particular way during the celebration of the Lord's Day.

Here Newman goes on to judge with much severity those frenetic and fanatical religious groups which had so much success in England in his day. It is not as though Newman condemns them *en masse*, but the distinction is clear: all those groups are to be rejected that say they follow an intense fervor but nevertheless *"detach themselves, more or less, from its [the Church's] discipline..."* (PPS III, 342).

There were frenetic persons also in the primitive

Church,[15] but God makes use of various means so as not to let them fall off the edge: miracles, meditation, mortification, the fear of God, persecutions, and that great school of exterior and interior discipline that is formal worship. No, one should not believe that dissident sects could be more fervent than the Church: their false fervor can be measured with serene and wise calm that the ceremonies of liturgical worship instill in the true faithful.

What follows is a very beautiful tribute to prayer as that true school and teacher of sanctity, most powerful before God and moreover a possibility for anyone at any moment: prayer for ourselves, prayer for the Church, prayer commanded by Christ Who wants to be our friend and to fulfill our desires.[16] Newman says: *"Thus, in both ways, whether our excitements arise from objects of this world or the next, praise and prayer will be, through God's mercy, our remedy; keeping the mind from running to waste; calming, soothing, sobering, steadying it; attuning it to the will of God and the mind of the Spirit, teaching it to love all men, to be cheerful and thankful, and to be resigned in all the dispensations of Providence towards us"* (PPS III, 349).

A misunderstood humanism can make us presume to obtain the same effects by our own will and intelligence alone, but Newman is ready to disabuse us of these illusions: *"Quarry the granite rock with razors, or moor the vessel with a thread of silk; then you may hope with such keen and delicate instruments as human knowledge and human reason to contend against those giants, the passion and the pride of man"* (Idea, 121).

---

[15] Here Father Velocci uses the word *"agitati."* It seems he is attempting to capture Newman's concern with those given to excessive emotionalism in religion, a concern echoed by Monsignor Ronald Knox a century later in his work *Enthusiasm.* — TRANS.

[16] See PPS III, 348–349.

What we would be if abandoned to ourselves is described in living color on a page of the sermon entitled "Mental Prayer";[17] and it is difficult for one who has read this sermon ever to forget it. But, fortunately, Christ has redeemed us, and the Holy Spirit, dwelling in us, strengthens us and enlightens us precisely by means of prayer.

Another effect of prayer is *separation from the world* and from slavery to it. Let us listen to Newman: *"Now the first great and obvious characteristic of a Bible Christian, if I may use that much abused term, is to be without worldly ties or objects, to be living in this world, but not for this world. . . . Now all this [elements of citizenship in the world] the Christian is in respect to Heaven. Heaven is his city, earth is not"* (SSD, 278).

Another characteristic of Christians described in the New Testament is prayer: *"In a word, there was no barrier, no cloud, no earthly object, interposed between the soul of the primitive Christian and its Saviour and Redeemer"* (SSD, 281). Is it not more than evident that here we find ourselves before a case of *post hoc, ergo propter hoc*, that is to say that it is precisely prayer that allows a Christian to obtain that separation from the world that is one of prayer's characteristics?

Furthermore, we have already seen how essential it is for one to attain such a result, in addition to private prayer, through public worship, with its fixed times and ceremonies that enliven the spirit.

A third effect of prayer exalted by the spiritual masters is *union with God.*

Newman is full of phrases like this, and we have just read one of them: *"no barrier, no cloud, no earthly object, interposed between the soul of the primitive Christian and its*

[17] See PPS VII, 208.

Saviour and Redeemer," an effect attributed to the spirit of prayer. We will now give at least another such expression, of particular force and solemnity: *"When men begin all the works with the thought of God, acting for His sake, and to fulfill His will, when they ask His blessing on themselves and their life, pray to Him for the objects they desire, and see Him in the event, whether it be according to their prayers or not, they will find everything that happens tend to confirm them in the truths about Him which live in their imagination, varied and unearthly as those truths may be. Then they are brought into His presence as that of a Living Person, and are able to hold converse with Him, and that with a directness and simplicity, with a confidence and intimacy,* mutatis mutandis, *which we use towards an earthly superior; so that it is doubtful whether we realize the company of our fellow-men with greater keenness than these favoured minds are able to contemplate and adore the Unseen, Incomprehensible Creator"* (GA, 117–118).

Another effect of well-practiced prayer is *our own interior transformation:* *"So a habit of prayer, the practice of turning to God and the unseen world, in every season, in every place, in every emergency (let alone its supernatural effect of prevailing with God),—prayer, I say, has what may be called a* natural *effect, in spiritualizing and elevating the soul. A man is no longer what he was before; gradually, imperceptibly to himself, he has imbibed a new set of ideas, and become imbued with fresh principles. He is as one coming from kings' courts, with a grace, a delicacy, a dignity, a propriety, a justness of thought and taste, a clearness and firmness of principle, all his own. Such is the power of God's secret grace acting through those ordinances which He has enjoined us. . . . As speech is the organ of human society, and the means of human civilization, so is prayer the instrument of divine fellowship and divine training"* (PPS IV, 230–231).

Such is the spiritualizing power of prayer, that in the Saints it is the immediate introduction to ecstatic union with God. Newman says this in regard to Saint Philip Neri: *"If he gave way to his habit of prayer in the most trifling degree, he immediately became lost in contemplation"* (MD, 97).

And there are still other effects of prayer: *"Now, at stated times, when we gather up our thoughts to pray, and draw out our petitions in an orderly and clear manner, the act of faith is likely to be stronger and more earnest; then we realize more perfectly the presence of that God whom we do not see . . ."* (PPS I, 251). Prayer reveals to us this hidden treasure that is God in us: *"Let us beg and pray Him day by day to reveal Himself to our souls more fully; to quicken our senses; to give us sight and hearing, taste and touch of the world to come"* (PPS VIII, 32). He also counsels: *"Let us then beg Him to teach us the Mystery of His Presence in us . . ."* (PPS V, 235); or in direct address to God, having recourse to Saint Monica: *"Gain for us, first, that we may intensely feel that God's grace is all in all, and that we are nothing . . ."* (Var., 14). Even the supreme gift of the love of God is sought and obtained by prayer: *"Let us pray God to give us* all *graces; and while, in the first place, we pray that He would make us holy, really holy, let us also pray Him to give us the* beauty *of holiness, which consists in tender and eager affection towards our Lord and Saviour . . ."* (PPS VII, 134).

The great gift which prayer can seek for us is also that of knowing the will of God: *"And, for that end, give me, O my Lord, that purity of conscience which alone can receive, which alone can improve Thy inspirations. My ears are dull, so that I cannot hear Thy voice. My eyes are dim, so that I cannot see Thy tokens. Thou alone canst quicken my hearing, and purge my sight, and cleanse and renew my heart. Teach me, like Mary, to sit at Thy feet, and to hear Thy word. Give me that true wisdom, which seeks Thy will by prayer and meditation, by direct intercourse with Thee, more than by reading and reasoning. Give me the discernment to know Thy voice from the voice of strangers, and to rest upon it and to seek it in the first place, as something external to myself; and answer me through my own mind, if I worship and rely on Thee as above and beyond it"* (MD, 380).

And analogously:

"Now, I will not judge another; I will not say that in this or that given case the fault of mind in question (for any how it is a fault), does certainly arise from some certain cause which I choose to guess at: but at least there are cases where this wavering of mind does arise from scantiness of prayer; and if so, it is worth a man's considering, who is thus unsteady, timid, and dim-sighted, whether this scantiness be not perchance the true reason of such infirmities in his own case, and whether a 'continuing instant in prayer,'—by which I mean, not merely prayer morning and evening, but some thing suitable to his disease, something extraordinary, as medicine is extraordinary, a 'redeeming of time' from society and recreation in order to pray more,—whether such a change in his habits would not remove them?" (PPS IV, 233).

As for the rest, our spiritual impotence is absolute, hence we have only prayer, so that God can set us free: *"Therefore, if we feel the necessity of coming to Christ, yet the difficulty, let us recollect that the gift of coming is in God's hands, and that we must pray Him to give it to us. . . . When then we feel within us the risings of this opposition to Christ, proud aversion to His Gospel, or a low-minded longing after this world, let us pray God to draw us; and though we cannot move a step without Him, at least let us try to move"* (PPS I, 213–214). With this means, we are sure of success because *"God does not command impossibilities. Therefore He gives us grace to raise us above our nature"* (SN, 191).

Other subjects or fruits of prayer are:

1. the truth of the Church and our perpetual union with her;[18]

---

[18] See MD, 378–380.

2. prayer for one's enemies, like the one composed by Newman at the time of the Achilli trial: *"God the lover and keeper of peace, grant peace and true love to all our enemies and give them remission of all their sins, and rescue us powerfully from their snares"*;[19]

3. or his act of celebrating a funeral Mass for Kingsley, who had so viciously attacked him: *"He was pleased to hear that Kingsley grew more orthodox with the years, and when he died in 1876, he said Mass for him"*;[20]

4. the request for particular lights to make an important decision, as Newman made at the time of his conversion to Catholicism: *"Continually do I pray that He would discover to me if I am under a delusion; what more can I do?"*;[21]

5. the great ecumenical gift of universal conversion: *"Enlighten all by Thy Holy Spirit; turning all Jews, Musselmen, and Pagans to Thee; converting all Atheists and Infidels, whether so in principle or practice; recovering all Heretics from the error of their ways, and restoring all Schismatics to Thy Holy Church; that there be one fold and one Shepherd, and sin with all its attendant misery may be banished from the earth"*;[22]

6. heavenly help in order to have trust in ecclesiastical authority even when they make us bitter or disillusioned: *"O my God, in Thy sight, I confess and bewail my extreme weakness in distrusting, if not Thee, at least Thy own servants and representatives, when things do not turn out as I would*

---

[19] Meriol Trevor, *The Pillar of the Cloud* (London: Macmillan, 1962), p. 571.

[20] Meriol Trevor, *Light in Winter* (London: Macmillan, 1962), p. 344.

[21] Anne Mozley, *Letters and Correspondence of J. H. Newman during His Life in the English Church* (London: Longmans & Green, 1911), vol. II, p. 412.

[22] Found in Vincent Ferrer Blehl's *Pilgrim Journey: John Henry Newman, 1801–1845* (London: Burns & Oates, 2001), p. 411. This prayer was contained in a notebook marked "most private and personal memoranda in two books (parts) 1805 to 1828."

have them, or expected! . . . O my dear Lord, give me a generous faith in Thee and in Thy servants!";[23]

6.1. the gift of using rightly one's reason: *"O gracious and merciful God, Father of Lights, I humbly pray and beseech Thee, that in all my exercises of Reason, Thy gift, I may use it, as Thou wouldst have me use it, in the obedience of Faith, with a view to Thy Glory, with an aim at Thy Truth, in dutiful submission to Thy Will, for the comfort of Thine elect, for the edification of Holy Jerusalem, Thy Church, and in recollection of Thine own solemn warning: 'Every idle word that men shall speak, they shall give an account thereof in the day of judgment; for by thy words, thou shalt be justified, and by thy words, thou shalt be condemned'"*;[24]

6.2. or, the grace to love one who has offended us and to pardon injuries: *"Can you pray that you may meet him [the one who had offended you] and love him in Heaven? You and he are both far from what you should be, and each has to* change. *Look on the* best *part of him. Think how he suffers. Purgatory useful for this—to bring you and him nearer to each other"* (SN, 246).

And the list could continue for pages and pages. But let us stop at this point, listening once again to the voice of Newman in a prayer that is almost a general overview of spiritual gifts that God can grant to a soul at prayer: *"Make me then like Thyself, O my God, since, in spite of myself, such Thou canst make me, such I can be made. Look on me, O my Creator, pity the work of Thy hands,* ne peream in infirmitate meâ—*'that I perish not in my infirmity.' Take me out of my natural imbecility, since that is possible for me, which is so necessary. Thou hast shewn it to be possible in the fact of the whole world by the most overwhelming proof, by*

[23] Ward, II, 365.
[24] Ward, II, 364–365.

taking our created nature on Thyself, and exalting it in Thee. Give me in my own self the benefit of this wondrous truth, now it has been so publicly ascertained and guaranteed. Let me have in my own person, what in Jesus Thou hast given to my nature. Let me be partaker of that Divine Nature in all the riches of Its attributes, which in fullness of substance and in personal presence became the Son of Mary. Give me that life, suitable to my own need, which is stored up for us all in Him Who is the Life of men. Teach me and enable me to live the life of Saints and Angels. Take me out of the languor, the irritability, the sensitiveness, the incapability, the anarchy, in which my soul lies, and fill it with Thy fullness. Breathe on me, that the dead bones may live. Breathe on me with that Breath which infuses energy and kindles fervour. In asking for fervour, I ask for all that I can need, and all that Thou canst give; for it is the crown of all gifts and all virtues. It cannot really and fully be, except where all are present. It is the beauty and the glory, as it is also the continual safeguard and purifier of them all. In asking for fervour, I am asking for effectual strength, consistency, and perseverance; I am asking for deadness to every human motive, and simplicity of intention to please Thee: I am asking for faith, hope, and charity in their most heavenly exercise. In asking for fervour I am asking to be rid of the fear of man, and the desire of his praise; I am asking for the gift of prayer, because it will be so sweet; I am asking for that loyal perception of duty, which follows on yearning affection; I am asking for sanctity, peace, and joy all at once" (MD, 430–431).

Conditions of Prayer

As our last point, let us look at the *conditions* of prayer. Not every prayer, in fact, is worthy of this name; not every prayer pleases God nor has the prerequisites to be heard by Him with benevolence. Newman says this time and again; we pray badly: *"And this is the highest excellence to which we ordinarily attain; to understand our own hypocrisy, insincerity, and shallowness of mind,—to own, while we pray, that we cannot pray aright..."* (PPS I, 147). And in the sermon on "Mental Prayer," Newman dedicates some space to a rather pessimistic analysis concerning the way people commonly pray, highlighting above all the disorder, the little attention, the egotistical interest, the scarce interiority with which we converse with God those few times that we do it.[25]

At any rate, it is absolutely necessary to correct the situation because prayer is a *sine qua non*, as Saint Alphonsus Liguori categorically affirmed: "Those who pray are certainly saved; those who do not pray are certainly damned."[26]

In Newman's sermon of December 14, 1837, dedicated to the effects of prayer,[27] after maintaining that prayer in all its forms (praise, thanksgiving, contemplation, petition) is a special privilege and duty of the Christian, he insists on the necessity of learning the most important art of praying: *"He who does not use a gift, loses it; the man who does not use his voice or limbs, loses power over them, and becomes disqualified for the state of life to which he is called. In like manner, he who neglects to pray, not only suspends the enjoyment, but is in a way to lose the possession, of his divine citizenship."* He goes on: *"Prayers and praises are the mode of his intercourse with the next world, as the converse of business or recreation is the mode in which this world is carried on in all its separate courses. He who does not pray, does not claim his citizenship with Heaven, but lives, though an heir of the Kingdom as if he were a child*

[25] See PPS, VII, 211ff.

[26] It is interesting that this same passage from St. Alphonsus is cited in the *Catechism of the Catholic Church* at no. 2744. —TRANS.

[27] PPS, IV, 226–238.

of earth" (PPS IV, 228). Newman uses this tone throughout this entire sermon. Therefore, to pray means to pray
much, to make of prayer a constant habit. But by observ-
ing what conditions?

Humility

For Newman, the conditions are the same as found in the
Roman Catechism or in Saint Alphonsus Liguori. Above
all is the condition of *humility: "We must pray in the spirit
and the temper of the extremest abasement, but we need not
search for adequate words to express this, for in truth no words
are bad enough for our case"* (PPS I, 147).

And so, Newman goes on to trace a perfect figure of
the ideal person who prays when he writes: *"Therefore,
when we pray let us not be as the hypocrites, making a show;
nor use vain repetitions with the heathen; let us compose ourselves, and kneel down quietly as to a work far above us,
preparing our minds for our own imperfection in prayer, meekly
repeating the wonderful words of the Church our Teacher, and
desiring with the Angels to look into them. When we call God
our Father Almighty, or own ourselves miserable offenders, and
beg Him to spare us, let us recollect that, though we are using a
strange language, yet Christ is pleading for us in the same
words with full understanding of them, and availing power; and
that, though we know not what we should pray for as we ought,
yet the Spirit itself maketh intercession for us with plaints
unutterable. Thus feeling God to be around us and in us, and
therefore keeping ourselves still and collected, we shall serve
Him acceptably, with reverence and godly fear; and we shall
take back with us to our common employments the assurance
that He is still gracious to us, in spite of our sins, not willing we
should perish, desirous of our perfection, and ready to form us
day by day after the fashion of that divine image which in
baptism was outwardly stamped upon us"* (PPS I, 147–148).

Trust

The second condition for prayer to be valid is *trust* that God hears us and can answer our prayers, even if we do not have material proof for these truths: *"Religious men cannot but feel, in various ways, that His Providence is guiding them and blessing them personally, on the whole; yet when they attempt to put their finger upon the times and places, the traces of His presences disappear. Who is there, for instance, but has been favoured with answers to prayer, such that, at the time, he has felt he never could again be unbelieving? Who has not had strange coincidences in his course of life which brought before him, in an overpowering way, the hand of God?"* (PPS VI, 248). Yet Newman observes: *"God does not so speak to us through the occurrences of life, that you can persuade others that He speaks. . . . God gives us enough to make us inquire and hope; not enough to make us insist and argue"* (250).

A picture of great delicacy and psychological truth, that suggests a just attitude of abandonment to God in one's prayer, is found in the character of the holy bishop featured in Newman's novel *Callista*: *"But the ways of the Most High are not as our ways, and those who to us seem nearest are often furthest from Him; and so our holy priest left the whole matter in the hands of Him to Whom he prayed, satisfied that he had done his part in praying"* (211). Why so much trust? Because one has faith: *"It is faith that is the appointed means of gaining all blessings from God"* (PPS I, 251). This assertion is immediately strengthened by the Gospel citation: "And Jesus said to him, 'If you can! All things are possible to him who believes' " (Mark 9:23).

Perseverance

Another condition for perfect prayer is *perseverance*. We have already seen, particularly in the sermon on "Mental

Prayer," that Newman recommends as a natural duty, beyond that of a divinely revealed commandment, prayer without ceasing, day after day, for our entire existence. If *"prayer is to spiritual life what the beating of the pulse and the drawing of the breath are to the life of the body"* (PPS VII, 209), it is clear that prayer which is not continuous and does not persevere until the end corresponds to the paralysis of the soul, and afterwards to its death.

In addition to the positive recommendations on persevering prayer, some of which we have already offered as a little anthology, now we would like to recall a negative portrait which preoccupied Newman and which he sketches of someone who prays with little or no perseverance; there is no better way to inculcate in us this condition for true and healthy prayer: *"Or supposing he has to repeat the same prayer for a month or two, the cause of using it continuing, let him compare the earnestness with which he first said it, and tried to enter into it, with the coldness with which he at length uses it. Why is this, except that his perception of the unseen world is not the true view which faith gives (else it would last as that world itself lasts), but a mere dream, which endures for a night, and is succeeded by a hard worldly joy in the morning?"* (PPS VII, 212).

A terrible perspective, against which Newman reacts by praying not only with perseverance, but also by having *the gift of final perseverance*, the greatest benefit that God could grant us: *"Oh, my Lord and Saviour, support me in that hour in the strong arms of Thy Sacraments, and by the fresh fragrance of Thy consolations. Let the absolving words be said over me, and the holy oil sign and seal me, and Thy own Body be my food, and Thy Blood my sprinkling; and let my sweet Mother, Mary, breathe on me, and my Angel whisper peace to me; that in them all, and through them all, I may receive the gift of perseverance, and die, as I decide to live, in Thy faith, in Thy Church, in Thy service, and in Thy love. Amen."* (MD, 290).

APPENDIX I

Prayers of John Henry Newman

JESUS THE HIDDEN GOD

Noli incredulus esse, sed fidelis.
Be not faithless, but believing.

I adore Thee, O my God, who art so awful, because
Thou art hidden and unseen! I adore Thee, and I desire to live by faith in what I do not see; and considering
what I am, a disinherited outcast, I think it has indeed
gone well with me that I am allowed, O my unseen Lord
and Saviour, to worship Thee anyhow. O my God, I
know that it is sin that has separated between Thee and
me. I know it is sin that has brought on me the penalty of
ignorance. Adam, before he fell, was visited by Angels.
Thy Saints, too, who keep close to Thee, see visions, and
in many ways are brought into sensible perception of
Thy presence. But to a sinner such as I am, what is left
but to possess Thee without seeing Thee? Ah, should I
not rejoice at having that most extreme mercy and favour
of possessing Thee at all? It is sin that has reduced me to
live by faith, as I must at best, and should I not rejoice in
such a life, O Lord my God? I see and know, O my good
Jesus, that the only way in which I can possibly approach
Thee in this world is the way of faith, faith in what Thou
hast told me, and I thankfully follow this only way which
Thou hast given me.

O my God, Thou dost over-abound in mercy! To live by
faith is my necessity, from my present state of being and
from my sin; but Thou hast pronounced a blessing on it.
Thou hast said that I am more blessed if I believe on
Thee, than if I saw Thee. Give me to share that blessedness, give it to me in its fullness. Enable me to believe as
if I saw; let me have Thee always before me as if Thou
wert always bodily and sensibly present. Let me ever hold
communion with Thee, my hidden, but my living God.

Thou art in my innermost heart. Thou art the life of my life. Every breath I breathe, every thought of my mind, every good desire of my heart, is from the presence within me of the unseen God. By nature and by grace Thou art in me. I see Thee not in the material world except dimly, but I recognise Thy voice in my own intimate consciousness. I turn round and say Rabboni. O be ever thus with me; and if I am tempted to leave *Thee*, do not Thou, O my God, leave *me*!

O my dear Saviour, would that I had any right to ask to be allowed to make reparation to Thee for all the unbelief of the world, and all the insults offered to Thy Name, Thy Word, Thy Church, and the Sacrament of Thy Love! But, alas, I have a long score of unbelief and ingratitude of my own to atone for. Thou art in the Sacrifice of the Mass, Thou art in the Tabernacle, verily and indeed, in flesh and blood; and the world not only disbelieves, but mocks at this gracious truth. Thou didst warn us long ago by Thyself and by Thy Apostles that Thou wouldest hide Thyself from the world. The prophecy is fulfilled more than ever now; but *I* know what the world knows not. O accept my homage, my praise, my adoration!—let me at least not be found wanting. I cannot help the sins of others—but one at least of those whom Thou hast redeemed shall turn round and with a loud voice glorify God. The more men scoff, the more will I believe in Thee, the good God, the good Jesus, the hidden Lord of life, who hast done me nothing else but good from the very first moment that I began to live.

THOU hast, O Lord, an incommunicable perfection, but still that Omnipotence by which Thou didst create, is sufficient also to the work of communicating Thyself to the spirits which Thou hast created. Thy Almighty Life is not for our destruction, but for our living. Thou remainest ever one and the same in Thyself, but there goes from Thee continually a power and virtue, which by its contact is our strength and good. I do not know how this can be; my reason does not satisfy me here; but in nature I see intimations, and by faith I have full assurance of the truth of this mystery. By Thee we cross the gulf that lies between Thee and us. The Living God is life-giving. Thou art the Fount and Centre, as well as the Seat, of all good. The traces of Thy glory, as the many-coloured rays of the sun, are scattered over the whole face of nature, without diminution of Thy perfections, or violation of Thy transcendent and unapproachable Essence. How it can be, I know not; but so it is. And thus, remaining one and sole and infinitely removed from all things, still Thou art the fullness of all things, in Thee they consist, of Thee they partake, and into Thee, retaining their own individuality, they are absorbed. And thus, while we droop and decay in our own nature, we live by Thy breath; and Thy grace enables us to endure Thy presence.

Make me then like Thyself, O my God, since, in spite of myself, such Thou canst make me, such I can be made. Look on me, O my Creator, pity the work of Thy hands, *ne peream in infirmitate meâ*—"that I perish not in my infirmity." Take me out of my natural imbecility, since that is possible for me, which is so necessary. Thou hast shewn it to be possible in the face of the whole world by the most overwhelming proof, by taking our created nature on Thyself, and exalting it in Thee. Give me in my own self the benefit of this wondrous truth, now it has been so publicly ascertained and guaranteed. Let me have in my own person, what in Jesus Thou hast given to my nature. Let me be partaker of that Divine Nature in all the riches of Its attributes, which in fulness of substance and in personal presence became the Son of Mary. Give me that life, suitable to my own need, which is stored up for us all in Him Who is the Life of men. Teach me and enable me to live the life of Saints and Angels. Take me out of the languor, the irritability, the sensitiveness, the incapability, the anarchy, in which my soul lies, and fill it with Thy fullness. Breathe on me, that the dead bones may live. Breathe on me with that Breath which infuses energy and kindles fervour. In asking for fervour, I ask for all that I can need, and all that Thou canst give; for it is the crown of all gifts and all virtues. It cannot really and fully be, except where all are at present. It is the beauty and the glory, as it is also the continual safeguard and purifier of them all. In asking for fervour, I am asking for effectual strength, consistency, and perseverance; I am asking for deadness to every human motive, and simplicity of intention to please Thee: I am asking for faith, hope, and charity in their most heavenly exercise. In asking for fervour I am asking to be rid of the fear of man, and the desire of his praise; I am asking for the gift of prayer, because it will be so sweet; I am asking for that loyal perception of duty, which follows on yearning affection; I am asking for sanctity, peace, and joy all at once. In asking for fervour, I am asking for the brightness of the Cherubim and the fire of the Seraphim, and the whiteness of all Saints. In asking for fervour, I am asking for that which, while it implies all gifts, is that in which I signally fail. Nothing would be a trouble to me, nothing a difficulty, had I but fervour of soul.

Lord, in asking for fervour, I am asking for Thyself, for nothing short of Thee, O my God, Who hast given Thyself wholly to us. Enter my heart substantially and personally, and fill it with fervour by filling it with Thee. Thou alone canst fill the soul of man, and Thou hast promised to do so. Thou art the living Flame, and ever burnest with love of man: enter into me and set me on fire after Thy pattern and likeness.

GOD THE BLESSEDNESS OF THE SOUL

TO possess Thee, O Lover of Souls, is happiness, and the only happiness of the immortal soul! To enjoy the sight of Thee is the only happiness of eternity. At present I might amuse and sustain myself with the vanities of sense and time, but they will not last for ever. We shall be stripped of them when we pass out of this world. All shadows will one day be gone. And what shall I do then? There will be nothing left to me but the Almighty God. If I cannot take pleasure in the thought of Him, there is no one else then to take pleasure in; God and my soul will be the only two beings left in the whole world, as far as I am concerned. He will be all in all, whether I wish it or no. What a strait I shall then be in if I do not love Him, and there is then nothing else to love! if I feel averse to Him, and He is then ever looking upon me!

Ah, my dear Lord, how can I bear to say that Thou wilt be all in all, whether I wish it or no? Should I not wish it with my whole heart? What can give me happiness but Thou? If I had all the resources of time and sense about me, just as I have now, should I not in course of ages, nay of years, weary of them? Did this world last for ever, would it be able ever to supply my soul with food? Is there any earthly thing which I do not weary of at length even now? Do old men love what young men love? Is there not constant change? I am sure then, my God, that the time would come, though it might be long in coming, when I should have exhausted all the enjoyment which the world could give. Thou alone, my dear Lord, art the food for eternity, and Thou alone. Thou only canst satisfy the soul of man. Eternity would be misery without Thee, even though Thou didst not inflict punishment.

To see Thee, to gaze on Thee, to contemplate Thee, this alone is inexhaustible. Thou indeed art unchangeable, yet in Thee there are always more glorious depths and more varied attributes to search into; we shall ever be beginning as if we had never gazed upon Thee. In Thy presence are torrents of delight, which whoso tastes will never let go. This is my true portion, O my Lord, here and hereafter!

My God, how far am I from acting according to what I know so well! I confess it, my heart goes after shadows. I love anything better than communion with Thee. I am ever eager to get away from Thee. Often I find it difficult even to say my prayers. There is hardly any amusement I would not rather take up than set myself to think of Thee. Give me grace, O my Father, to be utterly ashamed of my own reluctance! Rouse me from sloth and coldness, and make me desire Thee with my whole heart. Teach me to love meditation, sacred reading, and prayer. Teach me to love that which must engage my mind for all eternity.

M Y God I believe and know and adore Thee as infinite in the multiplicity and depth of Thy attributes. I adore Thee as containing in Thee an abundance of all that can delight and satisfy the soul. I know, on the contrary, and from sad experience I am too sure, that whatever is created, whatever is earthly, pleases but for the time, and then palls and is a weariness. I believe that there is nothing at all here below, which I should not at length get sick of. I believe, that, though I had all the means of happiness which this life could give, yet in time I should tire of living, feeling everything trite and dull and unprofitable. I believe, that, were it my lot to live the long antediluvian life, and to live it without Thee, I should be utterly, inconceivably, wretched at the end of it. I think I should be tempted to destroy myself for very weariness and disgust. I think I should at last lose my reason and go mad, if my life here was prolonged long enough. I should feel it like solitary confinement, for I should find myself shut up in myself without companion, if I could not converse with Thee, my God. Thou only, O my Infinite Lord, art ever new, though Thou art the ancient of days—the last as well as the first.

Thou, O my God, art ever new, though Thou art the most ancient—Thou alone art the food for eternity. I am to live forever, not for a time—and I have no power over my being; I cannot destroy myself, even though I were so wicked as to wish to do so. I must live on, with intellect and consciousness for ever, in spite of myself. Without Thee eternity would be another name for eternal misery. In Thee alone have I that which can stay me up for ever: Thou alone art the food of my soul. Thou alone art inexhaustible, and ever offerest to me something new to know, something new to love. At the end of millions of years I shall know Thee so little, that I shall seem to myself only beginning. At the end of millions of years I shall find in Thee the same, or rather, greater sweetness than at first, and shall seem then only to be beginning to enjoy Thee: and so on for eternity I shall ever be a little child beginning to be taught the rudiments of Thy infinite Divine nature. For Thou art Thyself the seat and centre of all good, and the only substance in this universe of shadows, and the Heaven in which blessed spirits live and rejoice.

My God, I take Thee for my portion. From mere prudence I turn from the world to Thee; I give up the world for Thee. I renounce that which promises for Him Who performs. To whom else should I go? I desire to find and feed on Thee here; I desire to feed on Thee, Jesu, my Lord, Who art risen, Who hast gone up on high, Who yet remainest with Thy people on earth. I look up to Thee; I look for the Living Bread which is in Heaven, which comes down from Heaven. Give me ever of this Bread. Destroy this life, which will soon perish—even though Thou dost not destroy it, and fill me with that supernatural life, which will never die.

THOU art the all-seeing, all-knowing God. Thy eyes, O Lord, are in every place. Thou art a real spectator of everything which takes place anywhere. Thou art ever with me. Thou art present and conscious of all I think, say, or do. *Tu Deus qui vidisti me*—"Thou, God, Who hast seen me." Every deed or act, however slight; every word, however quick and casual; every thought of my heart, however secret, however momentary, however forgotten, Thou seest, O Lord, Thou seest and Thou notest down. Thou hast a book; Thou enterest in it every day of my life. I forget; Thou dost not forget. There is stored up the history of all my past years, and so it will be till I die—the leaves will be filled and turned over—and the book at length finished. *Quo ibo a Spiritu Tuo*— "whither shall I go from Thy Spirit?" I am in Thy hands, O Lord, absolutely.

My God, how often do I act wrongly, how seldom rightly! how dreary on the whole are the acts of any one day! All my sins, offences, and negligences, not of one day only, but of all days, are in Thy book. And every sin, offence, negligence, has a separate definite punishment. That list of penalties increases, silently but surely, every day. As the spendthrift is overwhelmed by a continually greater weight of debt, so am I exposed continually to a greater and greater score of punishments catalogued against me. I *forget* the sins of my childhood, my boyhood, my adolescence, my youth. They are all noted down in that book. *There* is a complete history of all my life; and it will one day be brought up against me. Nothing is lost, all is remembered. O my soul, what hast thou to go through! What an examination that will be, and what a result! I shall have put upon me the punishment of ten thousand sins—I shall for this purpose be sent to Purgatory—how long will it last? when shall I ever get out? Not till I have paid the last farthing. When will this possibly be?

O my dear Lord, have mercy upon me! I trust Thou hast forgiven me my sins—but the punishment remains. In the midst of Thy love for me, and recognising me as Thine own, Thou wilt consign me to Purgatory. There I shall go through my sins once more, in their punishment. There I shall suffer, but here is the time for a thorough repentance. Here is the time of good works, of obtaining indulgences, of wiping out the debt in every possible way. Thy Saints, though to the eyes of man without sin, really had a vast account—and they settled it by continual trials here. I have neither their merit nor their sufferings. I cannot tell whether I can make such acts of love as will gain me an indulgence of my sins. The prospect before me is dark—I can only rely on Thy infinite compassion. O my dear Lord, Who hast in so many ways shown Thy mercy towards me, pity me here! Be merciful in the midst of justice.

GOD IS LOVE

Jesus saith to him, Lovest thou Me more than these?

THOU askest us to love Thee, O my God, and Thou art Thyself Love. There was one attribute of Thine which Thou didst exercise from eternity, and that was Love. We hear of no exercise of Thy power whilst Thou wast alone, nor of Thy justice before there were creatures on their trial; nor of Thy wisdom before the acts and works of Thy Providence; but from eternity Thou didst love, for Thou art not only One but Three. The Father loved from eternity His only begotten Son, and the Son returned to Him an equal love. And the Holy Ghost is that love in substance, wherewith the Father and the Son love one another. This, O Lord, is Thine ineffable and special blessedness. It is love. I adore Thee, O my infinite Love!

And when Thou hadst created us, then Thou didst but love more, if that were possible. Thou didst love not only Thy own Co-equal Self in the multiplied Personality of the Godhead, but Thou didst love Thy creatures also. Thou wast love to us, as well as Love in Thyself. Thou wast love to man, more than to any other creatures. It was love that brought Thee from Heaven, and subjected Thee to the laws of a created nature. It was love alone which was able to conquer Thee, the Highest—and bring Thee low. Thou didst die through Thine infinite love of sinners. And it is love, which keeps Thee here still, even now that Thou hast ascended on high, in a small tabernacle, and under cheap and common outward forms. *O Amor meus*, if Thou wert not infinite Love, wouldest Thou remain here, one hour, imprisoned and exposed to slight, indignity, and insult? O my God, I do not know what infinity means—but one thing I see, that Thou art loving to a depth and height far beyond any measurement of mine.

And now Thou biddest me love Thee in turn, for Thou hast loved me. Thou wooest me to love Thee specially, above others. Thou dost say, "Lovest thou Me more than these?" O my God, how shameful that such a question need be put to me! yet, after all, do I really love Thee more than the run of men? The run of men do not really love Thee at all, but put Thee out of their thoughts. They feel it unpleasant to them to think of Thee; they have no sort of heart for Thee, yet Thou hast need to ask me whether I love Thee even a little. Why should I not love Thee much, how can I help loving Thee much, whom Thou hast brought so near to Thyself, whom Thou hast so wonderfully chosen out of the world to be Thy own special servant and son? Have I not cause to love Thee abundantly more than others, though all ought to love Thee? I do not know what Thou hast done for others personally, though Thou hast died for all—but I know what Thou hast done specially for me. Thou hast done that for me, O my love, which ought to make me love Thee with all my powers.

THE PILLAR OF CLOUD

Lead, Kindly Light, amid the encircling gloom
    Lead Thou me on!
The night is dark, and I am far from home—
    Lead Thou me on!
Keep Thou my feet; I do not ask to see
The distant scene—one step enough for me.

I was not ever thus, nor pray'd that Thou
    Shouldst lead me on.
I loved to choose and see my path, but now
    Lead Thou me on!
I loved the garish day, and, spite of fears,
Pride ruled my will: remember not past years.

So long Thy power hath blest me, sure it still
    Will lead me on,
O'er moor and fen, o'er crag and torrent, till
    The night is gone;
And with the morn those angel faces smile
Which I have loved long since, and lost awhile.

At Sea
June 16, 1833

PRAISE TO THE HOLIEST IN THE HEIGHT

Praise to the Holiest in the height
   And in the depth be praise:
In all His words most wonderful;
   Most sure in all His ways!

O loving wisdom of our God!
   When all was sin and shame,
A second Adam to the fight
   And to the rescue came.

O wisest love! That flesh and blood
   Which did in Adam fail,
Should strive afresh against the foe,
   Should strive and should prevail;

And that a higher gift than grace
   Should flesh and blood refine,
God's Presence and His very Self,
   And Essence all-divine.

O generous love! That He who smote
   In man for man the foe,
The double agony in man
   For man should undergo;

And in the garden secretly,
   And on the Cross on high,
Should teach His brethren and inspire
   To suffer and to die.

          —from *The Dream of Gerontius*

AVE MARIS STELLA

Hail, Star of the Sea

TRULY art thou a star, O Mary! Our Lord indeed Himself, Jesus Christ, He is the truest and chiefest Star, the bright and morning Star, as St. John calls Him; that Star which was foretold from the beginning as destined to rise out of Israel, and which was displayed in figure by the star which appeared to the wise men in the East. But if the wise and learned and they who teach men in justice shall shine as stars for ever and ever; if the Angels of the Churches are called stars in the Hand of Christ; if He honoured the apostles even in the days of their flesh by a title, calling them lights of the world; if even those Angels who fell from Heaven are called by the beloved disciple stars; if lastly all the Saints in bliss are called stars, in that they are like stars differing from stars in glory; therefore most assuredly, without any derogation from the honour of our Lord, is Mary His mother called the Star of the Sea, and the more so because even on her head she wears a crown of twelve stars. Jesus is the Light of the world, illuminating every man who cometh into it, opening our eyes with the gift of faith, making souls luminous by His Almighty grace; and Mary is the Star, shining with the light of Jesus, fair as the moon, and special as the sun, the star of the heavens, which it is good to look upon, the star of the sea, which is welcome to the tempest-tossed, at whose smile the evil spirit flies, the passions are hushed, and peace is poured upon the soul.

Hail then, Star of the Sea, we joy in the recollection of thee. Pray for us ever at the throne of Grace; plead our cause, pray with us, present our prayers to thy Son and Lord—now and in the hour of death, Mary, be thou our help.

PRAYER FOR THE LIGHT OF TRUTH

I should like an enquirer to say continually:

O my God, I confess that *Thou canst* enlighten my darkness. I confess that Thou *alone* canst. I *wish* my darkness to be enlightened. I do not know whether Thou wilt: but that Thou canst and that I wish, are sufficient reasons for me to *ask*, what Thou at least hast not forbidden my asking. I hereby promise that by Thy grace which I am asking, I will embrace whatever I at length feel certain is the truth, if ever I come to be certain. And by Thy grace I will guard against all self-deceit which may lead me to take what nature would have, rather than what reason approves.

JESUS THE LIGHT OF THE SOUL

Mane nobiscum, Domine, quoniam advesperascit.
Stay with us, because it is towards evening.

I adore Thee, O my God, as the true and only Light! From Eternity to Eternity, before any creature was, when Thou wast alone, alone but not solitary, for Thou hast ever been Three in One, Thou wast the Infinite Light. There was none to see Thee but Thyself. The Father saw that Light in the Son, and the Son in the Father. Such as Thou wast in the beginning, such Thou art now. Most separate from all creatures in this Thy uncreated Brightness. Most glorious, most beautiful. Thy attributes are so many separate and resplendent colours, each as perfect in its own purity and grace as if it were the sole and highest perfection. Nothing created is more than the very shadow of Thee. Bright as are the Angels, they are poor and most unworthy shadows of Thee. They pale and look dim and gather blackness before Thee. They are so feeble beside Thee, that they are unable to gaze upon Thee. The highest Seraphim veil their eyes, by deed as well as by word proclaiming Thy unutterable glory. For me, I cannot even look upon the sun, and what is this but a base material emblem of Thee? How should I endure to look even on an Angel? and how could I look upon Thee and live? If I were placed in the illumination of Thy countenance, I should shrink up like the grass. O most gracious God, who shall approach Thee, being so glorious, yet how can I keep from Thee?

How can I keep from Thee? For Thou, who art the Light of Angels, art the only Light of my soul. Thou enlightenest every man that cometh into this world. I am utterly dark, as dark as hell, without Thee. I droop and shrink when Thou art away. I revive only in proportion as

Thou dawnest upon me. Thou comest and goest at Thy will. O my God, I cannot keep Thee! I can only beg of Thee to stay. *"Mane nobiscum, Domine, quoniam advesperascit."* Remain till morning, and then go not without giving me a blessing. Remain with me till death in this dark valley, when the darkness will end. Remain, O Light of my soul, *jam advesperascit!* The gloom, which is not Thine, falls over me. I am nothing. I have little command of myself. I cannot do what I would. I am disconsolate and sad. I want something, I know not what. It is Thou that I want, though I so little understand this. I say it and take it on faith; I partially understand it, but very poorly. Shine on me, *O Ignis semper ardens et nunquam deficiens!*— "O fire ever burning and never failing"—and I shall begin, through and in Thy Light, to see Light, and to recognise Thee truly, as the Source of Light. *Mane nobiscum*; stay, sweet Jesus, stay for ever. In this decay of nature, give more grace.

Stay with me, and then I shall begin to shine as Thou shinest: so to shine as to be a light to others. The light, O Jesus, will be all from Thee. None of it will be mine. No merit to me. It will be Thou Who shinest through me upon others. O let me thus praise Thee, in the way which Thou dost love best, by shining on all those around me. Give light to them as well as to me; light them with me, through me. Teach me to show forth Thy praise, Thy truth, Thy will. Make me preach Thee without preaching—not by words, but by my example and by the catching force, the sympathetic influence, of what I do—by my visible resemblance to Thy Saints, and the evident fullness of the love which my heart bears to Thee.

A PRAYER OF PRAISE TO THE HOLY SPIRIT, THE LIFE OF ALL THINGS

I adore Thee, my Lord and God, the Eternal Paraclete, co-equal with the Father and the Son. I adore Thee as the Life of all that live. Through Thee the whole material Universe hangs together and consists, remains in its place, and moves internally in the order and reciprocity of its several parts. Through Thee the earth was brought into its present state, and was matured through its six days to be a habitation for man. Through Thee, all trees, herbs, fruits, thrive and are perfected. Through Thee, spring comes after winter and renews all things. That wonderful and beautiful, that irresistible burst into life again, in spite of all obstacles, that awful triumph of nature, is but Thy glorious Presence. Through Thee the many tribes of brute animals live day by day, drawing in their breath from Thee. Thou art the life of the whole creation, O Eternal Paraclete—and if of this animal and material framework, how much more of the world of spirits! Through Thee, Almighty Lord, the Angels and Saints sing Thee praises in Heaven. Through Thee our own dead souls are quickened to serve Thee. From Thee is every good thought and desire, every good purpose, every good effort, every good success. It is by Thee that sinners are turned into Saints. It is by Thee the Church is refreshed and strengthened, and champions start forth, and martyrs are carried on to their crown. Through Thee new religious orders, new devotions in the Church come into being; new countries are added to the faith, new manifestations and illustrations are given to the ancient Apostolic creed. I praise and adore Thee, my Sovereign Lord God, the Holy Ghost.

O most Sacred, most loving Heart of Jesus, Thou art concealed in the Holy Eucharist, and Thou beatest for us still. Now as then Thou savest, *Desiderio desideravi*—"With desire I have desired." I worship Thee then with all my best love and awe, with my fervent affection, with my most subdued, most resolved will. O my God, when Thou dost condescend to suffer me to receive Thee, to eat and drink Thee, and Thou for a while takest up Thy abode within me, O make my heart beat with Thy Heart. Purify it of all that is earthly, all that is proud and sensual, all that is hard and cruel, of all perversity, of all disorder, of all deadness. So fill it with Thee, that neither the events of the day nor the circumstances of the time may have power to ruffle it, but that in Thy love and Thy fear it may have peace.

A SHORT VISIT TO THE BLESSED SACRAMENT
BEFORE MEDITATION

I place myself in the presence of Him, in Whose Incarnate Presence I am before I place myself there.

I adore Thee, O my Saviour, present here as God and man, in soul and body, in true flesh and blood.

I acknowledge and confess that I kneel before that Sacred Humanity, which was conceived in Mary's womb, and lay in Mary's bosom; which grew up to man's estate, and by the Sea of Galilee called the Twelve, wrought miracles, and spoke words of wisdom and peace; which in due season hung on the Cross, lay in the tomb, rose from the dead, and now reigns in Heaven.

I praise, and bless, and give myself wholly to Him, Who is the true Bread of my soul, and my everlasting joy.

ANIMA CHRISTI

Soul of Christ, be my sanctification;
Body of Christ, be my salvation;
Blood of Christ, fill all my veins;
Water of Christ's side, wash out my stains;
Passion of Christ, my comfort be;
O good Jesu, listen to me;
In thy wounds I fain would hide,
Ne'er to be parted from Thy side;
Guard me, should the foe assail me;
Call me when my life shall fail me;
Bid me come to Thee above,
With Thy Saints to sing Thy love,
      World without end. Amen.

—Translated

A PRAYER TO MARY, THE MOTHER OF JESUS

O Holy Mother, stand by me now at Mass time, when Christ comes to me, as thou didst minister to Thy infant Lord—as Thou didst hang upon His words when He grew up, as Thou wast found under His Cross. Stand by me, Holy Mother, that I may gain somewhat of thy purity, thy innocence, thy faith, and He may be the one object of my love and my adoration, as He was of thine.

O my God and Saviour, Who went through such sufferings for me with such lively consciousness, such precision, such recollection, and such fortitude, enable me, by Thy help, if I am brought into the power of this terrible trial, bodily pain, enable me to bear it with some portion of Thy calmness. Obtain for me this grace, O Virgin Mother, who didst see thy Son suffer and didst suffer with Him; that I, when I suffer, may associate my sufferings with His and with thine, and that through His passion, and thy merits and those of all Saints, they may be a satisfaction for my sins and procure for me eternal life.

A PRAYER FOR CHURCH UNITY

O Lord Jesus Christ, Who, when Thou wast about to suffer, didst pray for Thy disciples to the end of time that they might all be one, as Thou art in the Father, and the Father in Thee, look down in pity on the manifold divisions among those who profess Thy faith, and heal the many wounds which the pride of man and the craft of Satan have inflicted upon Thy people. Break down the walls of separation which divide one party and denomination of Christians from another. Look with compassion on the souls who have been born in one or other of these various communions which not Thou, but man hath made. Set free the prisoners from these unauthorised forms of worship, and bring them all into that one communion which thou didst set up in the beginning, the One Holy Catholic and Apostolic Church. Teach all men that the see of St. Peter, the Holy Church of Rome, is the foundation, centre, and instrument of unity. Open their hearts to the long-forgotten truth that our Holy Father, the Pope, is thy Vicar and Representative; and that in obeying Him in matters of religion, they are obeying Thee, so that as there is but one holy company in Heaven above, so likewise there may be but one communion, confessing and glorifying Thy holy Name here below.

O Lord Jesus Christ, upon the Cross Thou didst say: "Father, forgive them, for they know not what they do." And this surely, O my God, is the condition of vast multitudes among us now; they know not what they might have known, or they have forgotten what once they knew. They deny that there is a God, but they know not what they are doing. They laugh at the joys of Heaven and the pains of hell, but they know not what they are doing. They renounce all faith in Thee, the Saviour of man, they despise Thy Word and Sacraments, they revile and slander Thy Holy Church and her Priests, but they know not what they are doing. They mislead the wandering, they frighten the weak, they corrupt the young, but they know not what they do. Others, again, have a wish to be religious, but mistake error for truth— they go after fancies of their own, and they seduce others and keep them from Thee. They know not what they are doing, but Thou canst make them know. O Lord, we urge Thee by Thy own dear words, "Lord and Father, forgive them, for they know not what they do." Teach them now, open their eyes here, before the future comes; give them faith in what they must see hereafter, if they will not believe in it here. Give them full and saving faith here; destroy their dreadful delusions, and give them to drink of that living water, which whoso hath shall not thirst again.

A PRAYER FOR FAITHFUL SERVANTS
OF THE LORD

Blessed are they who give the flower of their days, and their strength of soul and body to Him; blessed are they who in their youth turn to Him who gave His life for them, and would fain give it to them and implant it in them, that they may live for ever. Blessed are they who resolve—come good, come evil, come sunshine, come tempest, come honour, come dishonour—that He shall be their Lord and Master, their King and God! They will come to a perfect end, and to peace at the last. They will, with Jacob, confess Him, ere they die, as "the God that fed them all their life long unto that day, the Angel which redeemed them from all evil;" [Gen. xlviii. 15, 16.] with Moses, that "as is their day, so shall their strength be;" and with David, that in "the valley of the shadow of death, they fear no evil, for He is with them, and that His rod and His staff comfort them;" for "when they pass through the waters He will be with them, and through the rivers, they shall not overflow them; when they walk through the fire, they shall not be burnt, neither shall the flame kindle upon them, for He is the Lord their God, the Holy One of Israel, their Saviour."

✓ A PRAYER FOR RELATIVES, FRIENDS, AND ENEMIES

O Jesus, Son of Mary, Whom Mary followed to the Cross when Thy disciples fled, and who didst bear her tenderly in mind in the midst of Thy sufferings, even in Thy last words, Who didst commit her to Thy best beloved disciple, saying to her, "Woman, behold thy son," and to him, "Behold thy Mother," we, after Thy pattern, would pray for all who are near and dear to us, and we beg Thy grace to do so continually. We beg Thee to bring them all into the light of Thy truth, or to keep them in Thy truth if they already know it, and to keep them in a state of grace, and to give them the gift of perseverance. We thus pray for our parents, for our fathers and our mothers, for our children, for every one of them, for our brothers and sisters, for every one of our brothers, for every one of our sisters, for our cousins and all our kindred, for our friends, and our father's friends, for all our old friends, for our dear and intimate friends, for our teachers, for our pupils, for our masters and employers, for our servants or subordinates, for our associates and work-fellows, for our neighbours, for our superiors and rulers; for those who wish us well, for those who wish us ill; for our enemies; for our rivals; for our injurers and for our slanderers. And not only for the living, but for the dead, who have died in the grace of God, that He may shorten their time of expiation, and admit them into His presence above.

PRAYER FOR A HAPPY DEATH

O H, my Lord and Saviour, support me in that hour in the strong arms of Thy Sacraments, and by the fresh fragrance of Thy consolations. Let the absolving words be said over me, and the holy oil sign and seal me, and Thy own Body be my food, and Thy Blood my sprinkling; and let my sweet Mother, Mary, breathe on me, and my Angel whisper peace to me, and my glorious Saints . . . smile upon me; that in them all, and through them all, I may receive the gift of perseverance, and die, as I desire to live, in Thy faith, in Thy Church, in Thy service, and in Thy love. Amen.

John Henry Newman: 1801–1890

John Henry Newman was born on February 21, 1801, in London. At Ealing School, he underwent a spiritual conversion which set him on the road to perfection. After undergraduate study at Trinity College, Oxford, he was elected Fellow of Oriel College. Ordained in the Church of England, he became Vicar of St. Mary's, in Oxford, where his spiritual influence on his parishioners and the undergraduates was enormous.

After 1833, he became the leader of the spiritual renewal known as the Oxford Movement. His studies of the Fathers of the Church led him to the conclusion that the Roman Catholic Church was the "One Fold of Christ." After a long interior struggle, he was received into the Catholic Church on October 9, 1845, by Blessed Dominic Barberi at Littlemore, where he had retired to live a semi-monastic life.

Ostracized by relatives and friends, he was ordained priest in Rome and returned to England to found in Birmingham the first Oratorian Congregation in England. This was followed by a second Oratorian house, in London. He became first rector of the Catholic University in Ireland and founded the Oratory School in Birmingham. In 1864, he published his *Apologia pro Vita Sua*, in which he vindicated his honesty in the Church of England and defended the Church of Rome.

He worked tirelessly for the poor of his parish, and carried on an enormous correspondence, helping count-

This brief biographical sketch is published with the permission of the Birmingham Oratory, which can be contacted for further information on the cause of Cardinal Newman's canonization.

less persons both Catholic and non-Catholic with their religious difficulties. He suffered much from the misunderstandings, suspicions, and opposition of some ecclesiastical authorities.

In 1879, Pope Leo XIII made him a cardinal, to the joy of all England. At his death in 1890, it was said that he more than any other person had changed the attitude of non-Catholics toward Catholics in England.

Cardinal Newman died in Birmingham on August 11, 1890; some fifteen to twenty thousand persons lined the streets as his body was borne to Rednal, eight miles away, for peaceful burial. The *Cork Examiner* affirmed, "Cardinal Newman goes to his grave with the singular honor of being by all creeds and classes acknowledged as the just man made perfect."

He was declared Venerable by Pope John Paul II on January 22, 1991.

Prayer for Cardinal Newman's Canonization

ETERNAL Father, You led JOHN HENRY NEWMAN to follow the kindly light of Truth, and he obediently responded to Your heavenly calls at any cost. As writer, preacher, counselor, and educator, as pastor, Oratorian, and servant of the poor, he labored to build up Your Kingdom.

Grant that through Your Vicar on earth, we may hear the words, "Well done, thou good and faithful servant, enter into the company of the canonized Saints."

May You manifest Your Servant's power of intercession by even extraordinary answers to the prayers of the faithful throughout the world. We pray particularly for our intentions in his name and in the name of Jesus Christ Your Son our Lord. Amen.